Sheheke
Mandan Indian Diplomat

The Story of White Coyote,
Thomas Jefferson, and Lewis and Clark

Tracy Potter

FARCOUNTRY
PRESS

Fort
Mandan
Press

Dedicated to the Mandan Nation.
He belongs to you.

For more information on Farcountry Press books:
Farcountry Press, P.O. Box 5630, Helena, MT 59604
or call (800) 654-1105 or visit www.farcountrypress.com

For more information on Fort Mandan Press and the
North Dakota Lewis & Clark Bicentennial Foundation:
Fort Mandan Press, P.O. Box 607, Washburn, ND 58577
or call (877) 462-8535 or visit www.fortmandan.com

Front cover: St. Memin's illustration of Sheheke. Courtesy of
The New-York Historical Society.
Back cover: Coyote photo courtesy of Donald. M. Jones.

Created, produced, and designed in the United States of America.
Printed in Canada.
ISBN 1-56037-253-2 (softcover)
ISBN 1-56037-255-9 (hardcover)

Sheheke.

Sheheke's wife, Yellow Corn.

Contents

Acknowledgments

The credit for this biography first and foremost goes to North Dakota. The state's rich history provided the data, and the way North Dakota raises its children inculcated the desire to mine the data and lent the skills to describe it.

The individuals who helped bring this book about are many and each important. My father, Alwyn, inspired by example a love of reading history and an appreciation for Louis L'amour, because L'amour wrote his stories from the ground up. The reality of the hills, stones, trees, and ridges meant something to L'amour and Alwyn. Then there were my instructors at the University of North Dakota, particularly D. Jerome Tweton and Glenn Smith, who presented history with such dignity and dry wit that it captured me and became my calling.

Smiling down from the wall above my desk is a photograph of Larry Remele, a constant inspiration whose premature passing left a gaping hole that other North Dakota historians are obligated to try to fill. Larry knew everything, it seemed—the only man of his time worthy of the title State Historian of North Dakota.

My mother, Doris Potter, who started college at age fifty-seven and became an ordained Presbyterian minister on her sixty-fifth birthday, provided inspiration, proving that it's never too late to start a new project. Good, intelligent friends Jim Fuglie and Eliot Glassheim gave honest

7

critiques that helped corral a book gone wild. Ev Albers, David Borlaug, Erik Sakareisen, and James Ronda all said very encouraging things and insisted that the book be published. Ev and Charlene Patterson both edited the manuscript. In the end it was David who stuck with the project and created Fort Mandan Press to get the book into print. Ken Rogers turned over his substantial file of research into Sheheke, providing leads and saving hours of study. Coralee Paul of St. Louis; Matt Muhlbaer, a graduate student at Temple University; and Sara Garland of Washington, D.C., tracked down research leads in St. Louis, New York, Philadelphia, and Washington. Nicole Wells of The New-York Historical Society helped puzzle out the St. Memin drawings of Sheheke and Yellow Corn. Bruce Donaldson of the Department of Cultural Resources for the province of Manitoba eagerly called on his own knowledge, his own research, and his wonderful network of Canadian historians to inform the book, as he has informed the author for many years.

Especially important to this study were the Mandan–Hidatsa people who answered annoying questions and listened patiently to the author's conclusions. Credit goes to Regina Schanandore, the Eagle Plume Woman of On-a-Slant Village; Keith Bear; Gerard Baker; Autumn Gwin; Calvin Grinnell; and Wanda Shephard, who took umbrage at hearing about the diplomatic relations between Americans and Mandans. "Aren't we Americans?" Wanda wondered. Three descendants of Sheheke-shote informed the author with probably too-brief conversations: Diane Medicine Stone, Darcy Medicine Stone, and Valerian Three Irons. Most helpful of all was Amy Mossett, a Mandan, a true friend and a scholar.

Thanks, too, to the Fort Abraham Lincoln Foundation board of directors who support and encourage preservation of the heritage of the Upper Missouri. Most of the research going into this project was done on their time as part of the interpretation of On-a-Slant Village within Fort Abraham Lincoln State Park. The state library, the Bismarck State College library, and the staff of the Elwyn Robinson Room in the Chester Fritz Library at the University of North Dakota all provided help.

My lovely Laura encourages all my work, and her confidence invades my doubts and gives me the inspiration to continue.

Thank you all.

Preface

The bicentennial commemoration of the Lewis and Clark Expedition is illuminating the rich multicultural history of the Missouri River Valley of North Dakota. Here is where, in 1804, Lewis and Clark built Fort Mandan, the first military outpost of the new Louisiana Territory, and spent an entire winter. They chose this place because it was the home of the Mandan and Hidatsa Nations, people whose reputation as friendly traders and hospitable hosts was already known to Thomas Jefferson when he issued his instructions to Meriwether Lewis.

Sparked by the bicentennial, great scholarship is resulting in bountiful articles, books, films, and other productions showcasing the story of the Expedition. The story of the native peoples who greeted Lewis and Clark may just be the most compelling chapter in the entire narrative.

Fort Mandan Press, under the auspices of the North Dakota Lewis & Clark Bicentennial Foundation, is pleased to launch a series of books devoted to revealing the richness of our region's heritage, with this volume by Tracy Potter. As only someone who truly understands the significance of this special part of our history can accomplish, Potter has woven a story as fascinating as any of the chapters that Lewis and Clark created on their epic journey. He takes us on another journey, beyond the Expedition—Sheheke's visit to President Jefferson.

In weaving this story, he also reveals the magnificence of the Mandan Indian culture. As Fort Mandan Press continues to tell the many stories of our special place, it will remain fitting that it all starts with Sheheke, one of the best friends of the new United States, who welcomed Lewis and Clark with the promise, "If we eat, you shall eat. If we starve, then you must starve also," forming a bond of friendship that not only endured through a long, cold winter, but for the ages.

David Borlaug, President
North Dakota Lewis & Clark Bicentennial Foundation

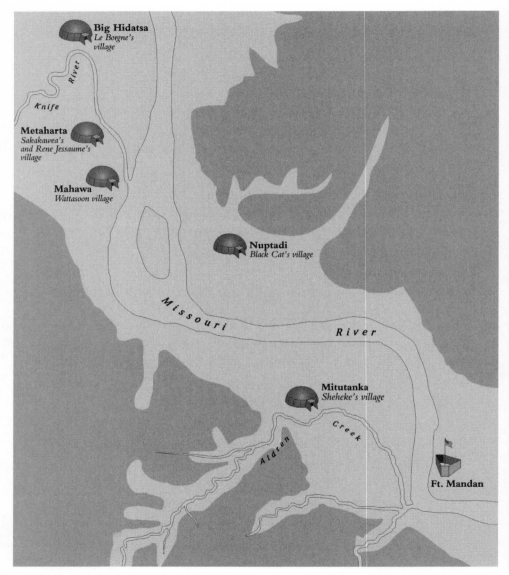

Knife River Indian villages in 1804.
COURTESY OF NORTH DAKOTA LEWIS & CLARK INTERPRETIVE CENTER

Introduction

The Mandan Indian Nation is the stuff of legends. The time of the Mandan's greatest eminence took place just before men with pens came much among them. There has, consequently, been less history and more hearsay, more archeological speculation than written-down memory. The first chroniclers more often reported what they'd heard about the Mandan than what they'd seen. Their reports were glowing. The Mandan were prosperous and peaceful people who were stalwart in defense of their lands. The earliest reports intimated that they were a tribe of white Indians, a legend that was easily tied to another legend about Welsh Indians, descended from a Prince Madoc, living in the interior of North America.

There are regrettably few eyewitness accounts of the Mandan in the golden age before their nation was smashed by repeated smallpox epidemics. By the time literate observation became more common, the Mandan were refugees, militarily dependent on their Hidatsa neighbors for security. The smallpox epidemic of 1781 struck at the fabric of the ancient culture. Not only did it drive them from their two-hundred-year-old Heart River villages and reorder their political situation, the smallpox also attacked the nation's memory. Coupled with the epidemic of 1837, a smallpox curtain was woven, obscuring the past. Oral tradition is a valuable historical resource—the first method of passing history through the generations—but its transmission in Mandan culture involved a strictly measured sequence of storytelling, involving years of training. Story D could only be taught to someone who had learned Stories A, B, and C. No story could be told to a person who had not yet earned the right to hear it. The time it took to teach the stories left knowledge of history vulnerable to the disruption caused by the epidemic.

Therefore, writing Mandan history is difficult. That might explain its dearth. It's not that the Mandan have been ignored. There have been wonderful studies of the Mandan, mostly by archeologists. Will and Spinden, Alfred Bowers, and Raymond Wood, among others, have done exceptional work in the area. Bowers and Wood wrote brief histories of the Mandan in works reflecting their archeological and ethnographic training. Bowers' doctoral dissertation, titled "A History of the Mandan and Hidatsa," arguably the best treatment of those peoples, was never published. Many others have written about the Mandan in connection with other earthlodge peoples or in relation to the Lewis and Clark Expedition.

There remains a book to be written, a focused and thorough history of the Mandan Indians, building on the historic record and the work of the archeologists, anthropologists, and oral historians. This is not that book, though it started out to be just that. It was hijacked.

As a device, just to get started and to provide some color and texture to the history, this manuscript opened with a ten-year-old boy awakening on an earthlodge in On-a-Slant Village in the summer of 1776. The boy was young White Coyote, Sheheke-shote, a real historical figure.

The choice was hard to avoid. He was a relatively famous Mandan whose life stretched across the first smallpox divide. He was the chief who traveled with Meriwether Lewis and William Clark to meet President Thomas Jefferson. His youth was lived in the well-studied (and well-known to the author) On-a-Slant Village during the last days of the zenith of his nation's history. The attempt to see the Mandan through the eyes of a Mandan of the past, though, could have worked with any character, even a fictional one. That would have saved a lot of trouble.

The device took over. Sheheke climbed down from his lodge roof and started doing things. He visited other villages, he went hunting, he watched his mother work, and worst of all, he began to carry on conversations. That was too much. It had become historical fiction. Helpful editorial suggestions guided it back to nonfiction.

But Sheheke had become too real. His story, too, needed to be told, thoroughly and in a timely manner. The bicentennial of his daring diplomatic mission draws near. A biography broke out.

So, rather than being a history of the Mandan utilizing one person as a foil, this book instead centers on that one person, necessarily placing the chief in his time and place. Instead of using one man to lend texture to a nation's history, the nation's history, at least up to 1812, was needed to help the biography make sense. Ethnographic information from Bowers and observers from closer to Sheheke's time, Prince Maximilian of Wied and George Catlin, give details and texture to the daily life of a Mandan man.

It is not particularly common to see a book-length biography of a man from a preliterate society. It is especially rare when the man isn't as prominent as Sitting Bull or Shaka Zulu. No journalist ever bothered to seek out Sheheke's friends and relatives to provide biographical background. Sheheke himself did not write, though he spoke some English and probably mastered other languages, including Plains Indian sign language. None of his friends wrote either, nor did any man of his acquaintance before his thirty-eighth birthday; at least none of his acquaintances before that time wrote anything about him. Much of his life-story is dependent on a scant family oral tradition and ethnographic information about other Mandan in other times. Neither of these is a completely reliable source, for obvious reasons. Family memory might be biased or confused. Ethnographic observation tends to generalize individuals and often provides only a snapshot in time, with the effect of generalizing moments, too. Fixed on the snapshot Catlin provides of the Game of the Arrow from his observation in 1832, we can only presume that the game was played like that in other times as well. It probably was, but there are other cases in which the culture was more dynamic and a single snapshot in time may give a false impression. Of course, very little in the study of history is certain at the best of times. Letters or documents may serve the purposes of their authors, whether for current benefit or historical positioning. Reports can be falsified. People sometimes lie. Historians, like archeologists, take what they can get.

In Sheheke's case what we get are snippets. He appears in the journals of Lewis and Clark and their sergeants, Ordway and Gass. Ensign Pryor talked to him. Alexander Henry met him. Pierre Chouteau and a Dr. Thomas observed him. John Bradbury and Henry Brackenridge did, too. President Thomas Jefferson spoke to him and wrote letters to him, though no record exists of what Sheheke said back to the American leader. John Luttig saw Sheheke. That's not much and there is very little else.

It is enough. The times he lived in were interesting and quite complex. In his life he saw smallpox devastate his entire culture. The whole Upper Missouri River country saw death on a scale unimaginable. He picked up the mantle of the leader who had united the stragglers and served as chief of his village. We know what has happened since then, with the advantage of hindsight. But the actors on the stage at that time didn't know the script. They were making the future. Sheheke was part of that play.

Others have told the story of the Mandan winter of 1804–05, beautifully and thoroughly, but not from this particular focus: one Mandan chief's involvement with the Corps of Discovery. His involvement was significant. Sheheke's support was pivotal in making the Americans welcome in the community of the five villages by the Knife River. He fed them, hunted with them, soldiered with them, agreed to follow what James Ronda has dubbed the American Policy, helped Clark make maps, and gave them information on subjects from Mandan origins to the politics and military situation of the Northern Plains. Though not their first choice, Sheheke was the one the Captains took back to the young nation's capital. His attempted return brought United States soldiers into mortal combat with Arikara warriors. His delayed but triumphant return to his people stirred up inter-village animosity. The tensions between the various village leaders are touched on in this book, in a way that draws sharper lines between the several bands of Mandan and Hidatsa than typically have been recognized. Historian Donald Jackson brought forward many significant documents about Sheheke's two attempts to go home in 1807 and 1809. This book brings those letters and reports together. Finally, it offers some analysis, a speculative attempt to make sense out of the last years of Sheheke's life.

Sheheke is an excellent representative of his nation. He was, like his nation, peaceful but willing to fight for a purpose. He had, like his nation, lived through thriving times and knew times of decline. He was, and his nation was, a consistent friend of the United States. Sheheke was a great American, from another nation. This is his story.

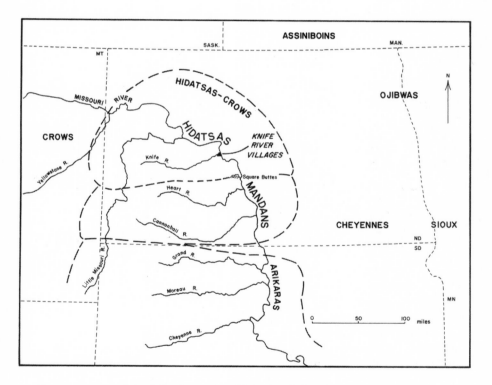

Resource areas of the Mandan and neighboring Indian nations circa A.D. 1700, just prior to the movement of the Cheyenne and Lakota Sioux bands to the Missouri River.

COURTESY OF *PEOPLE OF THE WILLOWS: THE PREHISTORY AND EARLY HISTORY OF THE HIDATSA INDIANS*

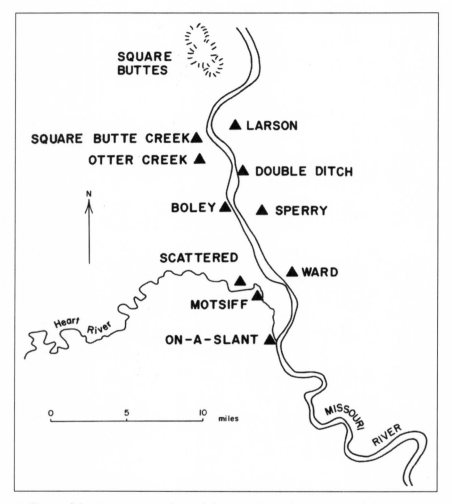

Villages of the Heart River Phase of the Mandan Indians. Seven of these ten sites were occupied during Sheheke's youth before the smallpox epidemic of 1781.

COURTESY OF *PEOPLE OF THE WILLOWS: THE PREHISTORY AND EARLY HISTORY OF THE HIDATSA INDIANS*

1

Born into a Golden Age

On-a-Slant Village might have been celebrating its bicentennial the year the boy who would become Sheheke (pronounced *Sha-heh-keh)*, White Coyote, was born. The thriving two-hundred-year-old village of a thousand or more Mandan Indians was located at the southern frontier of Mandan territory, just a few miles south of the mouth of the Heart River on the banks of the Missouri. It was 1766. To the Mandan people it was a Golden Age.

Forty years later, in the late summer of 1806, camped across the Missouri River from the ruins of On-a-Slant, Sheheke told Captains Meriwether Lewis and William Clark about the place of his birth.[1] The men were traveling together on a mission of peace and diplomacy that would take Sheheke to Washington, D.C., to a meeting with President Thomas Jefferson. It was a trip unprecedented in the history of his people.

Though the American captains had spent an entire winter as the neighbors and friends of the Mandan chief, though they had hunted and campaigned side-by-side, shared stories of their cultures, and made maps of the far and high country together, this conversation still required the aid of an interpreter, Rene Jessaume. And, though they knew Sheheke intimately as a friend and ally, they still got the translation of his name wrong. They called him Big White. That's how other contemporary writers knew him, too, and how history generally remembers him. Their Mandan interpreter, Jessaume, referred to him in French as *Le Gros Blanc*, that is, The Big White. Maybe the Americans didn't listen closely enough; Jessaume, who certainly knew the chief's name after a decade among the Mandan, should have introduced him as The Big White Prairie Wolf, probably *Le Gros Blanc Loup des Prairie*. The Captains also heard his name in the language of the Mandan as Sheheke-sh, a shortened version of his whole name. They apparently understood that the "sh" was not part of the name, but was an indicator of personhood. Coyote, the canine, is she-he-ke in Mandan. She-he-ke-sh is a man named Coyote. The Americans didn't record that Sheheke meant Coyote. Maybe they didn't know. Thomas Jefferson, fluent in French, understood Sheheke's name to be Wolf, which he probably got direct from Jessaume—the French had no word for coyote, an animal native to North America. His full name, the name by which he is still remembered among the people of the Three Affiliated Tribes— the Mandan, Hidatsa, and Arikara of the Fort Berthold Indian Reservation—is Sheheke-shote, or White Coyote.[2]

On the evening of August 18, 1806, after the camp was made and the fires set, Captain Clark sat down by Sheheke and inquired into Mandan traditions. Clark had heard some of the stories before, but he asked the chief to fill in the time frame for him. Clark wanted to know when the village opposite had been inhabited and what had been the cause of its abandonment. Sheheke reached far back, beyond history, to tell Clark how his people entered this world by climbing up a grapevine from their city under the earth. His recitation became solid history when it advanced into the period where Sheheke's memory took the place of his schooling in the oral traditions of the Mandan. He explained to Clark that there were seven villages of the Mandan in his youth, all as big or bigger than On-a-Slant. The Sioux and smallpox had killed most of his people; in their weakened condition, the Mandan had fled north, eventually forming into the two villages that Lewis and Clark knew. History does not record what other stories Sheheke might have told the men from the United States about his youth in On-a-Slant, but there are certainly more stories he could have told about his hometown. He could have told them that it ended its two-hundred-year history in flames.[3] On-a-Slant Village, *Miti O-pa-e-resh*, was founded before 1575[4] by families from three nearby villages where population was outstripping available garden space and wood resources. They came from the villages known as Boley and Motsiff[5], and *Mitoxte*, the Large and Scattered Village, which stretched for miles along the north bank of the Heart River from the Missouri deep into the area now occupied by the city of Mandan.[6] On-a-Slant was a planned community, chosen with an eye to its strategic location. It was also a frontier village, marking the southern edge of Mandan territory and providing protection from southern dangers for the villages farther north. Only the occasionally occupied village of the disgruntled, a temporary refuge for those engaged in village disputes, on Eagle Nose Butte, known by the Mandan as the Village of Those Who Quarrel,[7] was to the south of On-a-Slant.

In 1575, the most serious threats to Mandan communities came from the south. It had been that way for several hundred years. Intermittent wars with the Arikara, a people with a similar culture but from a different language stock, can be traced to the 1400s,[8] if not before. The centuries of sometimes genocidal warfare necessitated concern for defense. Village defenses discouraged theft, kidnapping, and murder by nomadic peoples, too. Protective walls and ditches became even more important when the Cheyenne and Lakota peoples moved to the Great Plains and adopted a light cavalry culture after 1700.

Mandan defensive systems were established early, probably before the twelfth century, and they didn't change significantly for seven hundred years. Log walls rose up from the interior slope of man-made ditches or natural features. The natural features recommended village siting at On-a-Slant.

At Miti O-pa-e-resh the only place an artificial ditch needed to be dug was on the western slope. On-a-Slant is a five-acre, roughly triangularly shaped piece of high ground with natural defenses on three sides. On the east, the Missouri River lay below a steep bank.

On the south, a deep ravine carved by seasonal melt and heavy rains made approach treacherous. The north side was a little less well protected, but a cutbank there gave village defenders the advantage of the high ground over any attackers. Only on the west, where a bluff rose above the earthlodges, was there a problem. The Mandan solved this problem with a massive public works project: the digging, with wood, stone, and bone tools, of a six-hundred-foot-long dry moat, five feet deep and, at first, about fifteen feet wide. Subsequent generations enlarged the ditch, expanding it outward on at least three occasions as garbage filled the ditches.[9] Two or more times the Mandan smudged the ditches by burning corn cobs in a layer covering the surface of the defensive channel. The ditch, besides its military function, probably served as a fire break, protecting the village from being caught up in a prairie fire. The periodic smudging would have served that purpose, too, in addition to any symbolic or ritual function it may have had.

High on the interior slope of the ditch, and likely around the entire circumference of the village, the Mandan placed a high log wall. Made mostly of cottonwood with mixed ash and elm, the walls rose ten or fifteen feet above the ditch. On the inside of the walls, the remainder of the excavated dirt formed a rampart, raising the defenders still higher above any potential attackers. When Pierre Gaultier, la Sieur de la Verendrye, became the first man of European descent to record a visit to the *Mantannes* in 1738, he declared the village defenses impregnable to other Indians. In fact, he said, the fortifications are not characteristic of the Indians.[10]

But of course they were. At least, they were characteristic of these Indians for centuries.

Within those walls, White Coyote could have told Lewis and Clark, there were eighty-five earthlodges, all owned by women, most containing between ten and twenty family members. The earthlodges were like the ones the Captains had seen in Mitutanka and the other villages. They were round and ranged in size from twenty to forty-eight feet in diameter. Inside and outside the lodges, and even outside the village walls, the earth was honey-combed with cache pits, covered-over root cellars that reached down in a bell shape five to seven and a half feet deep and four or five feet wide at the bottom. There were as many as nine pits under a single earthlodge, some in use holding previous seasons' harvests or deceased relatives, and some long-forgotten. The population of the village was between 1,000 and 1,500; most belonged to the Nuitadi, one of several identifiable bands in the loose confederation of Mandan villages. Of the seven villages in Sheheke's time, five on the west bank and two on the east,[11] On-a-Slant was the smallest. Yellow Earth Village, known today as Double-Ditch, was about twice as large. Altogether the population of the Mandan must have approached 15,000 persons.

On-a-Slant gets its name from its slope. From west to east the village drops pretty steadily about fifty feet in elevation over six hundred feet of distance from the west wall. Then a more level spot extends toward the river. Here the Mandan placed their ceremonial plaza and the *Mni-mih-douxx*, mistranslated into English as the Ark of the Lone Man, and also *Tixopinic*, the Medicine Lodge.

The plaza, the largest open area in the crowded urban center, was an oval half the length of a football field, about 160 feet from north to south and 90 feet from east to west. In the very center of the plaza stood the Ark, the name of which, Mni-mih-douxx, literally translates as Water-middle-mark, the shrine commemorating Lone Man's act that saved his people during the Great Flood. It is likely, given his eventual position of chief, that the earthlodge of Sheheke's youth, where he lived with his mother, Beaver Woman, and his father, White Pinto Horse,[12] was one of the thirteen surrounding the central grounds and looking in at the Ark. The principal families of the village lived along that inner circle.

There is an interesting question about the status Beaver Woman held in On-a-Slant. One branch of Sheheke's family tree believes that his mother was a white woman, either captured or rescued as a child after a raid in the Ohio River valley. Adopted Mandan could, and did, rise to prominence in the villages, but it would take a somewhat unusual set of circumstances for an adopted woman to come into ownership of an earthlodge. If the story of his mother's ancestry is correct, it is likely that Sheheke grew to adulthood in his grandmother's lodge or perhaps an aunt's lodge, an aunt he would have called his mother, just as he did his birth mother. The Mandan then, as today, could have several women they called mother.

The Medicine Lodge, Tixopinic, was also on the circle surrounding the ceremonial plaza. It was the only building in the village that wasn't round, and it was by far the largest, about ninety feet in diameter. It was, like the plaza, a public space. With its doorway facing into the plaza, straight at the Ark, the flat front of the Medicine Lodge was reminiscent of the long, rectangular lodges of centuries before in other, more ancient villages, such as Huff and Shermer, large cities between the Cannonball River and the Heart River that were abandoned by the Mandan before 1600. There were some rectangular lodges used in the early years of the deserted Chief Looking Village just across the river and upstream three miles. Looking Village, in the city of Bismarck, preceded On-a-Slant and was still occupied for most of Slant's history, but no one lived there during Sheheke's time. The earliest families there had chosen different methods for building their homes, some continuing the more ancient tradition of long houses and some trying a new style they had observed among the Arikara to the south. That style spread. By the time On-a-Slant was established all the lodges were built round, with the exception of the Medicine Lodge.

The Medicine Lodge had a different, more ancient look, and it had a more ancient and different mission than the family lodges. The big lodge was the only public building in the village, and it was the center of the city's religious, political, and social life. It was home to the medicine pipe, among other mysteries. The medicine pipe was powerful because it combined the energies of four medicine men simultaneously. It was ingeniously crafted out of clay with a large central bowl, a chamber where the smoke gathered, and four pipe stems to allow the four spiritual leaders to smoke together. Tixopinic was the place where the O-kee-pa and other national ceremonies came together.

The lodge was also used for meetings of the village council. Here great and lesser orations motivated the council and the city to actions for the good of the people. Sometimes the speeches called for war, to avenge a wrong or to defend their homes or their neighbors. Sometimes they were calls for public works, like the times the protective ditch had been redug and widened, or the many times the palisades had been restored. Sometimes, some of the best and most influential speeches had a different tone. It wasn't always as easy to whip up enthusiasm over simple sanitation issues.

There were very good, practical reasons for cooperation on sanitation. Epidemic diseases came more frequently to dirty villages and more seriously, as well. The nomads of the Great Plains, like the Lakota and Cheyenne, moved around, finding fresh water and clean places to set up their tepees. The Mandan, though, had chosen an urban way of life. Staying in a settled village, season after season for centuries, meant making and enforcing policies about proper waste disposal. The Mandan were a very clean people. The Missouri, though muddy, brought a constant supply of fresh water past the village. The Mandan took advantage of it by bathing daily, even twice a day, reputedly in all kinds of weather, though twenty below Fahrenheit probably slowed them down. Alexander Henry the Younger, head man of the North West Company on the Red River, was shocked in the summer of 1806 to see men and women bathing naked together and taking no notice of one another's nudity. Henry declared, "Modesty in the female sex appears to be a virtue unknown."[13] Like la Verendrye commenting on the fortifications, Henry was wrong. Modesty among Mandan women just took a form that he didn't recognize.

Away from the open plaza, the village was a crowded tangle of homes and winding streets. The earthlodges were all built in very similar fashions, with just a few variations. They ranged in size from a cozy twenty feet in diameter to over twice that.[14] Some had double entrances so a son-in-law would never have to meet his wife's or wives' mother face-to-face. Some had little apartments added on for more bed space. They were all constructed with four large central posts made from the trunks of cottonwood trees; usually there were thirteen surrounding posts sunk into the ground around the diameter of the lodge. Leaning logs were covered with willow bunches. A layer of sweetgrass or slough grass prepared the home for the final element: earth.

Born into a Golden Age

After a rain, when the earth was easy to cut, sod chunks about four inches square would be dug with buffalo-scapula hoes or levered out of the ground with fire-hardened wooden digging sticks. For a single lodge construction perhaps eight women would be recruited to dig the sod. Another twenty or so young women with several of their male suitors would carry the sod back to the village. Then the roofing material was placed on the lodge, grass side down, and pounded into place.[15] When the entire structure was covered to a depth of five or six inches, moistened clay would be rubbed on the outside, creating a kind of plaster that dried in the sun like adobe. Rain was its only enemy. After a heavy rainfall, women could be seen all over the village digging holes to find the proper plastering material, mixing water in, and patching the slumping lodges. Repeated slumping meant that the lower walls could be three feet thick.[16]

Like other Native American men on the Great Plains, Mandan men were primarily buffalo hunters. They took other game as well. In fact, archeological analysis indicates a shift over time from an overwhelming dependence on bison in the 1600s to a more balanced use of the resources locally available in the eighteenth century. Pronghorn antelope, white- and black-tailed deer, elk, and smaller animals fell to their arrows and musket balls. But hunting was what men did in every nation. What set the Mandan apart from nomadic tribes was the work of the women.

Beyond the village walls, down in the bottoms where periodic flooding refreshed the soil, were the rich gardens of the Mandan women. It was agriculture that made the Mandan rich. Corn was the major crop of the gardens, but each woman grew a variety of foods. In legend there were thirteen distinct varieties of corn grown by Mandan women, although only seven have come down to the present. There were, additionally, nine varieties of beans and five kinds of squash. There were also sunflowers.

The gardens were arranged by family, a collection of plots shaped to fill all the most productive niches. Most families' gardens were between 2,000 and 3,000 square feet. Some were squarish, while others were long and narrow rectangles. Others curved around natural formations or were tucked into points of land in whatever shape the Missouri allowed.

In mid-summer, when the crops were lush, the gardens were beautiful. Typically, a thin line of sunflowers surrounded a family's garden. Inside, the corn stood erect, more or less, while beans used the corn stalks for support. Squash spread out from its hills, covering wide patches of earth. Each crop blossomed according to its schedule, the sunflowers and squash producing the loveliest flowers. Diamond willow fences with heavy brush packed in below the bottom rails protected the gardens from straying horses, but dogs, children, and hunters were all needed at various times to save the growing foods from nocturnal visitors, particularly deer and raccoons. Deer bold enough to seek a meal in the gardens soon ended up as a meal in the lodges and as a new pair of moccasins or part of a buckskin dress.

Watcher platforms were scattered throughout the garden area. Here young boys would keep lookout while women and girls worked in the gardens. Without watchful eyes, garden work could be extremely dangerous. Women had little to fear from the wildlife of the Missouri region; typically not even prairie wolves were bold enough to attack people. Only grizzly bears ever threatened humans, and then only if attacked, or in the spring when the great light-colored bears were grouchy and hungry after waking up from their long winter hibernation.

The real danger was from other humans. The Cree, Dakota, Lakota, Cheyenne, Arikara, and the Assiniboine were all threats to unprotected women. So the boys kept watch, ready to alert the gardeners and the village's warriors if trouble crept up.

When the harvest was done, a woman's work wasn't. Food needed to be dried and stored away in cache pits. Stored food meant comfortable winters. It encouraged population growth. It also fueled trade.

Trade among Native American peoples has its roots in antiquity. Flint dug from quarries near Dunn Center, North Dakota, found its way across the continent. By the time of Christ, Knife River Flint, as it is known, had put in appearances as far north as Hudson Bay and southeast to the Carolinas and southwest to New Mexico. Obsidian made by Rocky Mountain volcanoes and shells from both coasts were also traded widely across the interior of North America. As Indian nations took up the hoe and started gardening in earnest, the nature of trade evolved. Where, formerly, trade had involved small, precious luxury items that might travel long distances, trade in foodstuffs was more regional in nature. Agricultural villages became established trading centers, reliable places for more nomadic peoples to visit. Those nomads generally circulated through the hinterlands of an agricultural people's region.

On-a-Slant was a cosmopolitan community in Sheheke's youth. Trade routes reached overland far to the west. Trading partners from that direction included the Arapaho, Cheyenne, and Crow. From the north came the Cree and Assiniboine, and, since 1738, white men, first the French and then the English. The Mandan had reputations as sharp traders and skillful linguists. The latter skill no doubt enhanced the former.

By the time of Sheheke's birth, horse culture was well-established among the Mandan. The first horses had arrived in the region by the 1730s. A group of Mandan children, kidnapped by the Cree and taken under the custody of one of la Verendrye's lieutenants, saw horses in Montreal in 1733. They told la Jemeraye that they had animals like that in their country. But there must not have been too many. When la Verendrye, at age fifty-one, walked from his Fort Rouge at modern-day Winnipeg to the Missouri in 1738, he failed to mention horses in his journal. He walked back to Canada. Four years later, however, when his sons walked to the Mandan villages, they rode from the villages to the plains beyond to the south.

Like other Indian nations, the Mandan were quick to adapt to riding. But as active traders, they also looked at the horse as a valuable item of exchange. The frontier of the horse, spreading north from Mexico from the 1500s and flourishing on the Great Plains, reached the Missouri about the same time as the frontier of the gun. Guns, powder, and ball may have preceded actual French-Canadian visits, but the availability increased dramatically with the opening of a steady trade with the north. As rare as horses were on the

Canadian prairies and North Woods lake country, that's how rare guns were on the plains south of the Mandan villages and in the Rockies to the west. The Mandan villages were a natural place for trades to take place. Mandan traders gained both guns and horses through the exchange.

Sheheke's education came from the open community school of his village. He learned by observation. He learned from his uncles and his peers. There was also some formal curriculum. Every boy over seven years of age showed up in the village plaza on war games mornings. They fasted that morning, so they came hungry to the plaza. Two experienced warriors divided the youngsters into two groups and then took them out on the prairie for training and maneuvers culminating in a big mock battle. The boys used real bows, but arrows of woven grass. Their scalps, too, were bits of grass. When one child shot another, the wounded boy was to lie down. The victor then put a moccasined foot on the victim's chest and took his grass scalp. After the battle, the young men, dead or alive, marched back into the village as heroes. The young girls of the village honored their return with a scalp dance. Both boys and girls were practicing the moves they had learned by observing adult behavior.

While still a boy, Sheheke participated in group buffalo hunts. He became a hunter himself through frequent practice and under the easy tutelage of his uncles and older peers. Again, observation was the key learning tool. He played the game of the arrow, with some relevance in training for hunting, but more particularly a preparation for battle. Men and boys alike gambled at the game, which had very simple rules. A contestant shot an arrow as high into the air as possible and then notched and shot one after another as rapidly as he could. The winner was the one who had the greatest number of arrows in the air at the same time.

At about age ten, Sheheke entered his first age-grade society, a group recalled variously as the Dogs Whose Names are Not Known, or as the Foolish Dogs. A modern analogy might be to the Boy Scouts, where fifth graders mingle with high school boys in one club. He would have graduated about his fifteenth year, which was right around the time that smallpox came to On-a-Slant. After the Foolish Dogs, boys generally took some years off from membership in any society. Then, when they were adults there were more choices of societies available.

Sheheke learned his history in two ways. First was storytelling. The Mandan told their stories six months of the year. It was inappropriate the other six months.[17] Instructional stories trained a person to assume responsibility for a bundle, both an actual physical bundle of artifacts and mementos, and a bit of the cultural oral tradition of the nation. There was a proper order in which stories could be learned. It was a wonderfully complex and democratic system of maintaining a history, a process imbuing history with importance simply by the serious and paced method of teaching. But it was a system with a fatal flaw, as 1781 and 1837 pointed out. The smallpox curtain must have fallen on hundreds of significant stories when there was no time for them to be passed on in the proper way. When four of five people die in a matter of weeks, and an aspect of the society requires slowness in the transmission of cultural heritage, a lot of culture can be lost.

Secondly, Sheheke learned by observation. The O-kee-pa ceremony was a four-day extravaganza of dance and self-sacrifice with great significance for the well-being of the village. It can also be looked on as a national history festival. There was Everything Comes Back Day when all the legendary and mythical figures of the Mandan come back to the village. The whole panoply of characters: *Hoita*, the Speckled Eagle who had once imprisoned all living things at Dog Den Butte; and Lone Man, who had freed them, were there; along with the shocking Foolish One and dozens of dancers dressed to represent eagles, holy women, swans, snakes, hawks, beavers, meat, night and day, wolves, coyotes, meadowlarks, and pronghorn antelope.[18]

One of the major purposes of the O-kee-pa was to bring fertility to the buffalo herds. It was an outcome fraught with peril, however. An evil spirit, the *O-ke-hee-de*, alternately known as The Owl or The Foolish One came to the village during the ceremony intent on procreation and impressively equipped for the task. The women had to be protected and The Foolish One overcome and directed into doing the bidding of the Mandan.

The O-kee-pa was held each summer to ensure that buffalo would be abundant and to guarantee general good fortune to the village. Some years, as many as three such ceremonies would be held, if there were that many eager O-kee-pa-Makers available. It was a great honor, and responsibility, to make an O-kee-pa. Not just anyone could do it.

If a man had received a vision of buffalo singing the songs of the O-kee-pa, he could apply to village council members for their permission to make an O-kee-pa, to be named *Kani-Sachka*. It was largely a consensus decision, because the Maker would need a lot of help. It was a big commitment of resources.

The council members involved in deciding were those who had the special portfolio of picking young men to aid in the O-kee-pa. If enough of them agreed to help, the Maker's family started gathering goods for the event. Every lodge in the village was happy to donate something since every lodge would benefit from the proper observance of the ritual. Most of the things collected would be redistributed to the men helping put on the ceremony.

At dawn on the morning before the O-kee-pa began, many eyes kept a watch beyond the village walls. From far off over the prairie a single figure came into view. It was *Numakmax Ena*, Lone Man, a fact shouted throughout the lodges. Dogs, feeling the excitement of their human friends, added their voices to the chaos. Their masters rounded the dogs up. Dogs and the youngest children were confined to their lodges for a time. But others were not. The lodge roofs filled with villagers.

Lone Man made a direct line to the village and entered. The men of the Black Mouth Society stopped him, as they would any stranger, and questioned him. He had come from his home on a high hill to the south, he said, so that the O-kee-pa lodge could be opened for the coming ceremonies.[19] The Black Mouths escorted Lone Man directly to the chief's lodge. There he met with some of the leading men of the village in ritual consultation. He spoke in a variation of the Mandan language that was old when On-a-Slant was new. Lone Man weaved the tribe's history together with his own. He told of a battle with Hoita, the Speckled Eagle, over a white buffalo robe, of the Great Flood, of how he had given the Mandan turtles, cedar, and the O-kee-pa ceremony itself.

After the meeting, Lone Man made a circuit of the village, reciting history as he went. When he stopped at the lodges of the eight young men who would be attending the Kani-Sachka, families of the young men gave Lone Man prized knives. He noted which came from whom so that the proper knife would be used later on the proper young man. Then, he made his way to the Medicine Lodge and performed a ceremony, opening it for the O-kee-pa. Lone Man, his duty done for the evening, then took his leave of the headmen and returned to the prairie, slipping over the same butte from which he had come.[20]

On the first night of the O-kee-pa, the Maker took all his collections to the Medicine Lodge. He stood in the rear center of the lodge behind an altar flanked by human and buffalo skulls. Singers and their drums were by the door. The Lone Man was with them. He had his wooden medicine pipe, one of the nation's most significant relics. The Medicine Lodge was built, like the other lodges, with the door facing the Ark of the Lone Man. The altar was set where the Maker could peer over the central hearth through the doorway and see the Ark in the center of the plaza. He would be able to see many young men coming from the plaza. They would fast during the four days, trying to prove worthy of acquiring some *xo'pini* to give them success as hunters and warriors. The young men came naked to the lodge, carrying their finest bow-cases, fanciest quivers, and their fathers' medicine bundles. They arranged themselves around the inside wall of the lodge by their clan divisions. They would not eat for four days.

Lone Man had presented his pipe to the Maker, along with his wishes for a correctly performed ceremony. The first night the Maker was not responsible for the services, however. Hoita directed things inside the lodge. He oversaw a dance, the conclusion of which, in the middle of the night, set the young men to crying. They cried all night.[21]

At sunrise, the Kani-Sachka took over. As much of the village watched from the rooftops of the earthlodges, the O-kee-pa Maker came out of the Medicine Lodge and walked to the Ark of the Lone Man. He was wearing only a loin-cloth of buffalo skin. He was painted entirely yellow and had a wreathe of white buffalo fur around his head. Kani-Sachka went to its south side and grabbed a plank. He called to Lone Man's post inside the shrine and asked him to hear his prayers. He prayed for the people to have all they asked for, to bring the buffalo near, and to keep all bad luck away.

Six older men carrying the sacred turtle drums came out of the lodge, three striking them upriver and three down. Singing started inside the Medicine Lodge. Attention shifted from the praying Maker to the door of the lodge. Four pairs of select young men, fasters all, danced out shaking their O-kee-pa rattles while dressed as buffalo and covered with fresh willow bundles. They were naked below the skins. They were each painted black with two long red stripes running from waist to shoulder and continuing to wrists and ankles. White bands ran across each dancer's chest and paralleled the red line on his legs and arms. They danced while the Maker prayed, his head leaning on the Ark of the Lone Man. The pairs danced out to the Ark, four men on each side. Then each group of four circled the plaza in opposite directions, ending back at the Medicine Lodge.

Sheheke undoubtedly watched the dancers intently. He would also be a buffalo dancer some day. The young learn by observation. They learn best by careful observation.

As they danced near the Ark, the young buffalo would rise up and bellow at each other. Some closely imitated the movements and sounds of a bull in rut. The dancers then surrounded Kani-Sachka, dancing close and spreading their robes to cover him. They separated and spun out in their groups of four, reconvening around the turtle drum group. Then they returned to the Medicine Lodge. There the buffalo faced each other, four on each side of the opening, heads inclined and hands outstretched with the robes forming an archway into the lodge. The turtle drums were carried through the arch, and the four pairs of dancers followed it into the Medicine Lodge. The pattern was repeated three more times during the day. After the

Born into a Golden Age

fourth dance, the Lone Man walked to the Medicine Lodge with the turtle drums in his arms. If the drums seemed heavy, it was a sign, Sheheke and the other villagers knew, that there were buffalo herds nearing the village. The nearer the buffalo, the heavier the drum.

The next morning, while the O-kee-pa Maker prayed by the Ark, the Lone Man wandered the village carrying his medicine pipe. Families thankful for the blessings of Numakmax Ena presented him with buffalo robes. Meanwhile, the young fasters in the O-kee-pa lodge were becoming buffaloes. Some of them were painted to prepare for another day of dancing as buffalo, while the others fought like young male buffaloes in rut. Just past noon, the painted dancers emerged from the lodge, dancing their way to the Ark. The other fasters, wearing buffalo robes, came out of the Medicine Lodge and formed a line to aid the Maker's prayers. When the fasting young men returned to Tixopinic, some would be readied for self-sacrifice they were about to undergo, while others continued to improve their painting and their costuming.

The third day of the O-kee-pa was the most exciting. It was a costumed history lesson, Everything Comes Back Day. When George Catlin observed the ceremony in 1832, he said at least thirty young men participated, representing the many animals and legendary creatures mentioned previously. The Foolish One made his appearance on the third day. His shocking appearance sent the girls and women of the village into fits of more-or-less good-natured terror. All through the earlier days, challenges had been shouted from the village, daring The Foolish One to show up and test his medicine against the powers of Lone Man and the sacred pipe. Finally, on the third day and after the first dance of the day by all the other legends, The Foolish One came into sight zigzagging his way across the prairie and over the hills to the village gate.

The Foolish One was painted black and was nearly nude, but for some tufts of buffalo hair around his ankles and waist. He had a buffalo's tail and enormous genitalia. Two pumpkins hung below a giant fake penis that was connected by a thin piece of sinew to an eight-foot-long rod he carried. He used the rod to raise his member, threatening the women of the village with it and sending them into fits of mock terror. Chaos gripped the village until the evil creature reached the ceremonial plaza. Then the Kani-sachka restored order.

With the medicine pipe in front of him, the O-kee-pa Maker confronted The Foolish One, upbraiding him for disrupting the ceremony and frightening the people. All attention, naturally, was drawn to the two characters and the whole village fell silent while the spiritual struggle took place. As The Foolish One wilted under the power of the pipe, the village erupted into a victory song. The Foolish One, unable to stand against the Kani-sachka, the pipe, and the song of a unified village, changed his focus from the women to the buffalo dancers. He acted like a bull in rut and even attempted to mate with one of the dancers. His final, fatal mistake came when he attempted to enter the Medicine Lodge. Evil creatures come to no good end at the door to the Tixopinic. The Foolish One's rod broke at the door. That signaled the women to first taunt and then attack him: ". . . one snatches his wand from his hands and breaks it across her knee - his power is then gone, and he is pelted from all sides with handsful of yellow dirt, under the shower of which he darts through the crowd, and escapes from the village through the picket onto the prairie."[22] The women ripped his costume from him; as he ran from the village, his genitalia was wrapped like a doll and paraded around the plaza, finally coming to rest attached to a pole in front of the Medicine Lodge, offered as a sacrifice to the first Foolish One, who resides in the sun.

Throughout the last three days of the O-kee-pa, the Mandan observed one of the best known traditions of Plains Indians. Other Siouan peoples allow or encourage their young men to carry out self-sacrificial ceremonies. In modern parlance this practice is generically referred to as the Sun Dance. Among the Mandan, the event was wrapped up in the O-kee-pa. Many of the young men fasting in the Medicine Lodge, and finally the Kani-Sachka on the fourth day, presented themselves for the test of bravery, piety, and endurance. Sharp blades cut the skin of the warriors' chests. Skewers of wood were woven under the skin, and by those skewers the men hung from the cross-beams of the Medicine Lodge. Weights—either buffalo skulls tied to their legs, or if the faster had killed an enemy, an enemy's skull hung around his neck—increased the discomfort.

While the men hung in the lodge, on the fourth day, the turtle drums beat for success in buffalo hunting. Four men dressed as buffalo bulls danced four times around the Ark. The bulls then sang to the four directions. To the north, the song was for the winter hunt. To the east, spring buffalo were called. The south and west singers called out to the summer and fall herds, respectively. Then, the grand finale of the four-day event occurred. When the faster became unconscious, he would be taken down from the rafters and awakened. As the last song to the buffalo ended, and with buffalo skulls tied to the skewers, the men would emerge from the Medicine Lodge and begin to dance, walk, or be helped around the plaza, plodding forward one foot at a time, until the skulls pulled the skewers from their skin, or they lost consciousness again. The dancers would be taken to a sweat lodge to recover their strength.

The last act of the O-kee-pa was the distribution of gifts. The officers and attendants of the ceremony were presented with the things the Kani-Sachka and his family had collected over the months of preparation. All was distributed, with one exception. The knives used on the brave young men were thrown away, tossed into the Missouri as an offering to Grandfather Snake, the river spirit.

Each time the O-kee-pa ceremony was performed, Sheheke and the other youth were able to watch the young men carry out their various roles. He learned in this way the history of the people, and he learned how to take his place in it.

Mandan boys and girls learned to swim in the dangerous currents of the Missouri. George Catlin commented on their skill, noting that the Native American swimming method differed from that of European men. Mandan swimmers did not use the breast stroke, then the method generally employed by whites, according to Catlin. They used the more powerful and speedier stroke now referred to as the Australian crawl.

> The Indian, instead of parting his hands simulta-
> neously under the chin, and making the stroke out-

ward, in a horizontal direction, causing thereby a
serious strain upon the chest, throws his body alternately upon the left and the right side, raising one
arm entirely above the water and reaching as far forward as he can, to dip it, whilst his whole weight
and force are spent upon the one that is passing
under him, and like a paddle propelling him along;
whilst this arm is making a half circle, and is being
raised out of the water behind him, the opposite
arm is describing a similar arch in the air over his
head, to be dipped in the water as far as he can
reach before him, with the hand turned under,
forming a sort of bucket, to act most effectively
as it passes in its turn beneath him.[23]

That stroke came in handy in the search for Missouri marinade.
Every spring, as the Missouri broke up and ice flows started moving
down the river, buffalo floated along too. Some had tried walking
on thin ice and had fallen in. Some were still alive. Some had been
dead for a very long time. These were the favorites of the Mandan.
Long-dead and formerly frozen buffalo, chilled in iced snowmelt,
was considered a delicacy. It was probably the stolen-apple effect,
where something tasted better just because it was hard to get. These
floating buffalo were hard to get. Young men, with the whole village
cheering them on, would leap from shore to ice carrying a lariat, as
they did on the first day of April, 1836, near Mitutanka. Francis
Chardon, proprietor of the fur trade post at Fort Clark, recorded
the scene in his journal.

> Friday 1st — Calm beautiful day. Ice running
> very thick in the River — The Indians had great
> Sport in catching buffalo that was floating down on
> the ice — a few were still living having taken their
> Station on large masses of ice — traveled very
> quickly down Stream. But the greater part that was
> hauled on Shore had been previously drowned. It is

Born into a Golden Age

astonishing the feats of hardy dexterity that was performed by some of the Young Men in pursuit of the
loathsome Meat. They would boldly embark on the
first piece of floating ice that approached the Shore,
and Springing from piece to piece - or - swimming
when the distance was too great to leap, would generally succeed in fastening a cord round the horns
— and towing the carcase to shore.

This scene, reported by other commentators in other years, says
a lot about the state of Mandan youth. Brave, strong, and confident
men who were a little foolish risked their lives against the Missouri
on April 1. Hardy men, too, adapted to a crisp climate, or they
wouldn't have the strength to climb out of the water and onto the
next floe. Young men of Sheheke's generation were more than
adapted to their position along the Missouri in the Golden Age of
the Mandan; they were born and bred to be Mandan. And the
Mandan youth of the spring of 1781 were set to inherit a rich and
productive domain with a proud and ancient tradition to maintain.

2

Two Histories of the Mandan

The Mandan first moved to the banks of the Missouri River in what is now eastern South Dakota around A.D. 650, according to prevailing archeological theory. They migrated from northwestern Iowa or southwestern Minnesota where their characteristic culture had evolved. When they emigrated to the Missouri valley, they were not in a competition for agricultural land. They were the first in their region to make a transition from a woodland-era hunting and gathering tradition to one that relied more heavily on cultivated products of the garden.

Before A.D. 1100, there were two distinct groups of Mandan populating the Missouri from central South Dakota to central North Dakota. The two groups, while similar in cultural traits, apparently had some differences. They fought. The northern Mandan won and occupied most of the area for more than a century.[24]

A shift in climate at the beginning of the thirteenth century, the Pacific I climate episode characterized by archeologist Donald Lehmer as an increased flow of dry westerlies into the Northern Plains, chased the northern Mandan back to the somewhat cooler summers of North Dakota. For the next two centuries the Mandan planted crops and villages in the country above the Grand River and below the Square Buttes, the boundary of Hidatsa territory. Then, around 1450, Pacific I blew itself out. With more favorable conditions, population grew, and the Mandan reacted in two ways.

They established the largest villages in their entire history, like the heavily fortified site of Huff, in the country above the Cannonball River, and they moved back south of the Grand, into central South Dakota. But the area they re-entered wasn't empty. Their cousins, the people they had previously defeated, remained and had been joined by the Arikara. The Arikara, a Caddoan-speaking people closely related to the Pawnee, had pioneered corn cultivation on tributaries of the Missouri in western Nebraska. Pacific I made those areas untenable and the marginal Caddoans had moved east to the Missouri. The Missouri was heavily occupied in Nebraska, however, and the Arikara drifted north in the thirteenth century into the area only lightly held after the retreat of the northern Mandan.

So, when the northern Mandan returned in the 1400s, they found significant opposition. There was more warfare. This time the northern Mandan seem to have lost to the Arikara and the southern Mandan disappeared entirely, either through acculturation or extermination.[25]

The northern Mandan, now the only Mandan, retreated. For a century, up to about 1550, they defended their large, heavily fortified villages as far south as the Cannonball River. By 1600, however, they had consolidated into the area between the Heart River and the Square Buttes. That was about the time they shifted from long, rectangular lodges to more lumber-efficient round construction. The people in the two villages on the east side of the Missouri were of the *Nuptadi* band. The ones on the west were *Awigaxa* and *Nuitadi*. None of the groups had always been in the region of the Heart River.

That's the story, more or less, of archeologist Donald Lehmer's analysis of the Middle Missouri cultural traditions. It is not universally accepted, and it is never proposed straight-up with word usage like northern Mandan, southern Mandan, and Arikara. Archeologists don't write that way, but this is what Lehmer alluded. This is, however, not the Mandan's own story of how they got to the Heart River. There are two of those.

The tribe arose from the earth, the Mandan origin stories agree. Some place that entry on the west bank of the mighty Mississippi River near its delta on the Gulf of Mexico. Others believe that they emerged along the banks of the Missouri, just a little south of On-a-Slant. In either case, the origins of the Mandan began underground.

The Mandan lived in a huge village under the surface of the earth. Through a hole in the earth, a grapevine grew down, stretching all the way to the Mandan village.[26] Naturally, the vine drew attention. As their eyes followed the grape vine up and up, they noticed a spot of light far above them. Some brave adventurers climbed to the light. Emerging onto the earth, the explorers found vast numbers of buffalo and other game. They found plums and grapes. They gathered up some of the bounty and returned home. When the villagers below tasted the grapes, they were impressed. They decided to go up the vine and live upon the face of the earth. Great numbers of men, women, and children climbed the vine and came out on the surface. But, while many were still waiting their turns, a very large woman, big-bellied, perhaps with child, tried climbing the vine. It couldn't hold her and collapsed, trapping much of the tribe in their subterranean village. To some of the Mandan, the underground village was where they returned when they died.[27] The place where the underground village opened onto the crust of world was, as previously mentioned, a matter of some dispute. Some thought it was near the Heart River. There were quite a number of significant sacred places in the Heart River region.

Those that believed the place of origin was far to the south had an epic migration story to go with the belief. It was a steady, measured odyssey that brought them north. Led by three brothers and their sister the Mandan people left their point of origin and began a long, slow journey north. They were farmers, even then, and they would stop along the journey to plant and harvest corn crops. They did not live in earthlodges during the migration, but were content to build temporary homes like those used by later generations on eagle-trapping expeditions to the Bad Lands. Temporary lodges were just right for temporary villages, better than carrying tepee poles and hides, or, alternatively, investing time and energy in the construction of more permanent homes.

The migration involved carrying things. In the years before the horse, the Mandan, like other Native American nations, had dog travois. They're not very big, though, and it takes a lot of dogs to move a lot of stuff. A single dog couldn't haul a tepee. The Mandan, by reputation, did not keep as many dogs as some other peoples, the Hidatsa, for instance. The ability to transport things on the odyssey was limited. Given the choice between carrying food and building temporary shelters from locally obtainable materials and carrying shelters while seeking food, the Mandan chose to carry food.

When the Mandan reached the place where the Missouri meets the Mississippi, their journey could continue in three directions. They could head northwest along the Missouri, cross the Missouri, or cross the Mississippi. They chose to cross over to the east bank of the Mississippi. The tribe marched north along the Mississippi, the legend continues, until it was no longer so mighty and the deciduous forests gave way to conifers. Placing that tree change on a map, the prairie of southern Minnesota gives way to a deciduous forest in a transitional zone closely related to the line of Interstate 94 through the state. The deciduous forest is a pretty narrow band, yielding to the boreal forest on a line parallel to the prairie-forest transition, say from Itasca State Park in the northwest toward Mille Lacs on the St. Croix River.

Itasca State Park is the defined beginning of the Mississippi. It's a beautiful place dotted with burial mounds of woodland era peoples. It might have been fine for harvesting the natural products of the forest, but it was, and is, poor country for gardening and worse for mosquitoes. The headwaters of the Mississippi are today defined as being there, but the Mandan may not have seen it that way. Their migration could have taken them up the east bank of the St. Croix when they reached its confluence with the Mississippi. That would bring the Mandan to the boreal forest 150 miles or so south and east of Itasca.

The northern forests were not good for corn farming, so the

Mandan turned south and west, eventually settling for a time by the pipestone quarries, the source of the red rock so highly prized by other Indian nations. Pipestone, or catlinite, was the stone of choice for the making of pipe bowls over a wide range of the Great Plains and northern forests. The Mandan weren't particularly fond of the pipestone, though. To them it seemed to signify blood, not appropriate for ceremonial smoking. Unlike most of their neighbors, the Mandan molded their medicine pipes out of clay. Working in clay allowed the pipemakers a great deal of artistic expression.[28] There were certainly some pipestone pipes in Mandan villages in the 1800s, and probably long before, but never so many as among other nations. The Mandan used medicine pipes of pottery, like the one which never left the Medicine Lodge and was smoked by four spiritual men simultaneously. There were at least two medicine pipes completely carved from wood. One was used in the Corn Ceremony, the other in the O-kee-pa to frighten O-kee-he-de, the Evil Spirit.[29]

If the Mandan migration story can be related to archeological theory, Pipestone is the place where it begins to come together. If the Mandan are in the region of southwestern Minnesota in the mid- to late-seventh century, then researchers have to look earlier to find them in central Minnesota, or in Missouri, or on the Gulf of Mexico. Archeologists and historians would be surprised to find gardeners in the forests of Minnesota, A.D. 600, or earlier. But the Mandan story says they figured that out, too. They could see it was not a good place for gardeners.

Pushing back even farther, is it at all possible that the Mandan were growing crops during their epic journey? It might be. Peter Nabokov and Dean Snow write that squash was cultivated in Kentucky before 1000 B.C., and maize, it is believed, was in the southwestern United States by A.D. 200, possibly brought north by corn advocates, missionaries from Mexican corn cultures.

The Mandan origin on the west bank of the Mississippi, way down at its mouth, seems incredible. But the Siouan language stock spread wide. From Virginia to Louisiana and from Lake Superior and the Assiniboine River to the Gulf of Mexico there were Siouan peoples, like the Mandan. If the Mandan had become aware of themselves as a people where the legend starts, they would have been frontier Siouan speakers, pressured from the west by Caddoan speakers. Migrations can start for reasons like that.

While at Pipestone, forty lodges of the Awigaxa band separated from the rest of the nation and drifted north to the region of the Red River and its tributary, the Sheyenne. They were above the Sheyenne to the north of Devils Lake when a flood encouraged them to move southwest, where they found the Missouri and settled in the Heart River region.

While the others still lived at Pipestone they were visited by Lone Man and the First Creator. They learned many ceremonies from the two great culture heroes. One day a buffalo hunting party ranged far to the west and rediscovered the Missouri. The tribe moved west and settled in villages along the Missouri, at the mouth of the White River. Here they were taught the O-kee-pa, the principal ceremony of the tribe. It had originally been an Arikara ritual, but those farmer-warriors from the south with their Caddoan language had never been able to make much of it, having only a single dancer to call the buffalo. (This portion of the tradition relayed by Alfred Bowers from his interviews with Mandan and Hidatsa elders in the 1920s is disagreed with vehemently by descendants of Nuptadi Mandan who say that the O-kee-pa has always been part of Mandan culture and that the Arikara, relative late-comers to the Upper Missouri, receive too much credit for influencing Mandan culture.) The Mandan had perfected the dance into a four-day, village-wide event. The Arikara were given the Prairie Dog Curing Ceremony in exchange.

Eventually Lone Man and First Creator convinced most of the people to go north and join their Awigaxa cousins by the Heart.[30] The bottomlands by the mouth of the Heart were rich and better suited for farming, they said. Winter buffalo herds sheltered there, too.

The Nuptadi and Nuitadi began another northern migration, this one in small increments, building villages and planting gardens all along the way. Eventually they reached the region north of the

Cannonball River up to the Heart, where they were reunited with their long-lost relations. They established some very large villages. Shermer, on the east bank, was a place where certain remembrances and ceremonies took place even four hundred years or more after its abandonment.[31] Even after the centuries had passed and the walls around the village had fallen, it was still possible to find the central plaza and see the way the streets had been laid out in very straight lines. Shermer was known as the Village Where Turtle Went Back. A sacred turtle who lived in the Missouri near there was the central figure in some of the ceremonies. Across the river from Shermer, the Huff Village was another example of the large cities of Sheheke's ancestors; it was protected by a defensive scheme even more serious than the one in use later at On-a-Slant. Piquets, sharpened poles angled out of the inner wall of the ditch, gave a ferocious look to the defenses, if not much more.

The remaining bands of the Awigaxa, tradition says, tried life to the west of the Missouri, settling on small tributary streams running out of the Black Hills. After a tragic event where many lodges of families of the Awigaxa disappeared while hunting buffalo for sinew on the south side of the Black Hills, the remainder of the band established fortified villages back on the Missouri south of the Cannonball, near the mouth of the Grand River. When the Great Flood came, the reunited northern Mandan gathered by the Heart and were protected there by Lone Man and the sacred cedar. The people at the Grand did not have the sacred cedar. Some villagers stayed and drowned. Others, fleeing the flood, escaped to the Rocky Mountains. The survivors attempted to raise corn in mountain valleys, but seasons there were too short. When they returned to the Grand, they found the Arikara had claimed the area, so the last element of the Mandan people headed north to the Heart River region, settling between the other Mandan bands and their Hidatsa neighbors to the north.

Once there, however that might have happened, the Mandan of the Heart River Phase were lords of a productive and thriving domain, though it may not have been a very large one. Just fifteen miles, as the crow flies, separated the southernmost village, On-a-

Slant, from the northernmost, Larson. Their hunting range, naturally, stretched far beyond the towns, reaching out across the buffalo-filled plains to the east of the Missouri and west to the North Dakota Bad Lands. Within the fifteen miles of Missouri riverside, the land was turned over to intensive agriculture. Family garden plots averaging a couple acres in size produced more than sufficient amounts of corn, squash, and beans. The Mandan traded surpluses to more nomadic peoples for meat, hides, and luxury items from the seashore and the mountains. In time, horses, metal tools, and guns and gunpowder were obtained for corn and hides.

The two-hundred-year-long Heart River Phase saw an accelerating pace of change. While the Mandan seem to have achieved more of a balance with their available wood and productive land resource than at any comparable stretch in their history, the introduction of European goods and the disruption brought by the colonial powers set in motion changes that made a Mandan village of 1775 a remarkable place compared to the same village of 1575. The changes, particularly in the last hundred-year period up to 1775, would have been more amazing to a Mandan time traveler than the accumulated transformations of the previous five hundred years. Most obvious was the introduction of the horse because of the way it improved mobility and speeded communication. The horse changed the nature of the hunt. It also changed warfare. Its possession by other Indians meant that nomadic enemies became much more dangerous.

That change, the advent of more dangerous nomads, was perhaps a more significant one than the arrival of the horse to the Mandan. In hindsight it appears that the acquisition of the horse made the nomadic lifestyle so attractive that people abandoned the river valleys, the forests, and the lakes and headed for the open plains, where they thrived with the new "technological" innovation. In fact the availability of the horse was just a very happy coincidence for the Lakota people who were disrupted from their traditional lives by the cascade effect put in motion by white influence on the margins of their homelands. To risk over-generalizing the subject, it is accurate to say that pressures from French Canada drove the Lakota, also known as the Tetons or Western Sioux, from Minnesota. As tribes confronted the French, they either accommodated them and became trading partners, thereby obtaining guns and ammunition, or they opposed the French and faced a protracted struggle. When the French moved, the Indian nations were put into motion. The Cree, Assiniboine, and Ojibway traded with the French more often than they opposed them. The Indians of the northern forests consolidated a hold on Minnesota; they won an arms race, at least initially, with the Dakota and Lakota people. The Dakota bands mostly remained in southern Minnesota or on its margins. The Lakota, who were familiar with the Dakota plains as a hunting region, moved across the prairie to the Missouri around 1700. As they became a horse culture, they thrived; within a few generations, they created a Northern Plains empire from Kansas to Montana at the expense of the nations who had been resident there for centuries.

The increasing power of the Lakota, and also the Cheyenne, who left their gardens and earthlodges along the James River to take up life in the Black Hills region, was not so great as to bring sieges and destruction of earthlodge villages before 1781. The villages were still islands of security, where hospitality and trade reigned. The more immediate effects were felt in hunting, where long excursions to the Bad Lands or the prairies became more dangerous. Trade was also affected. As John Jackson put it, "The great threat to the river people was a large population of Sioux pressing from the east and Assiniboine warriors attacking the supply route from the west and north. After horses improved mobility, the danger increased."[32]

Whether or not the Mandan of the 1700s understood that the geopolitical changes they were observing had white people at their root, they certainly knew that guns and ammunition and metal tools came from the whites, even if they came through Indian middle-men, like the Assiniboine. The Mandan were sharp traders. They knew that middlemen are costly and that trade would best be pursued directly with the whites. When la Verendrye came in 1738, they greeted him in the manner of an honored guest. The Mandan have continued to treat white visitors well to the present day.

As 1781 dawned, the Mandan lived in seven villages, five on the west side of the Missouri and two on the east. On the west, from south to north, are seven old village sites from the Heart River Phase: The temporary village at Eagle Nose Butte, On-a-Slant, Motsiff, Large and Scattered, Boley, Square Butte Creek and Otter Creek. It is suspected by Stan Ahler, who dug a site under the city of Mandan in 1999, that Large and Scattered was abandoned early in the eighteenth century.[33] If that is so, and Sheheke wasn't counting Eagle Nose Butte, the other five are the ones about which he told Clark. On the east side of the river were Yellow Earth, now known as Double Ditch, a state historic site that recent digging indicates dates back to the Huff era of the fifteenth century,[34] and Larson. The Looking Village above River Road in Bismarck, a site of the transition from rectangular to round earthlodges, is thought to have been abandoned before Sheheke's time, too. The three distinct groups of Hidatsa were north of the Mandan, running from the Painted Woods area to the north bank of the Knife River, where the only semi-sedentary Hidatsa Proper had established Big Hidatsa Village, known to them as Menetarra. The Awaxawi Hidatsa, often referred to as the Wattasoons or Amahaways, who had come to the Missouri earlier than the Hidatsa Proper and who had been more thoroughly acculturated into a Mandan-type lifestyle, lived in the Painted Woods area. The Awatixa, neighbors of the Mandan for six hundred years or more, are harder to place. They likely occupied one or more villages between the Awaxawi and the Hidatsa Proper.

The population of the ten or more villages was probably between 20,000 and 25,000 persons.[35]

The gardens were healthy and regularly produced nutritious grains and vegetables, more than could be eaten, and so surpluses protected against famine and fueled trade. Game was plentiful. Refined hunting techniques brought protein, clothing, and tools to the earthlodges. Wood was a scarce resource, but that was a fact of life to which the Mandan had long-since adapted. A balance with nature had been found that allowed their cities to prosper for two hundred years on the same ground. Their trade network stretched overland to the north and northeast, and west and southwest. It brought the traditional luxury items from far away and a wonderful, diverse flow of ever more useful manufactured items from the Canadians. They had healthy horse herds and were well armed compared to their neighbors. Their ancient culture was respected and its rituals practiced. Life was, in Sheheke's youth, for the most part, very good.

3

Good Things from the Whites

Working with porcupine quills is hard. First, a porcupine is needed, preferably dead. The Mandan and Hidatsa, among other tribes, had elaborate eagle-trapping rituals that sometimes included the plucking of feathers from live and dangerous birds. No one has recorded quill removal ceremonies from live porcupines. The quills are sharp and barbed. Working with them leads even the most skilled to get lots of little punctures. The quills need to be separated from the porcupine, flattened between the artist's teeth, and dyed before they are ready to be woven into works of art and attached to clothing, painted robes, and pipestems.

This centuries-old tradition faced stiff competition when European goods became available in North America. Long before the first white man walked or paddled into what became North Dakota, his products were available at the trading centers of the Mandan Indians. Beads made it to the Missouri by 1600 or so.[36] Pre-formed glass beads made pretty decorations, and they were a lot easier to deal with than quills. Small, light, and easy to transport, beads led the way in bringing the world of the colonial powers to the world of the continent's interior.

An ancient trade route started bringing European goods to the villages late in the seventeenth century. Long before that, Mandan traders had walked northeast across the broad buffalo prairie first finding, and then keeping, the Turtle Mountains to their left. They crossed the Pembina River and struck north to the Assiniboine. The 250-mile-long trail took the Mandan traders to a place known to the early fur traders as Portage la Prairie.[37]

At Portage la Prairie, the merchants of the Missouri met the people of the woods and canoes. The canoes of the northern tribes worked an interconnected waterway that reached to Hudson Bay. When, in the late 1600s, European ships appeared on the southwestern shore of Hudson Bay, the trade at the southern end of that series of rivers and lakes began to include iron tools, guns, and powder.[38]

La Verendrye reached the same area by a different route. His network stretched back east from Portage la Prairie through the woods and lakes of Manitoba and along the north shore of the Great Lakes and St. Lawrence River all the way to Montreal. The route was different, but the goods were the same. The existence of two routes, however, would play a role in maintaining fair prices for Mandan goods right up to the time of Lewis and Clark.

In the creation of wearable art, adding decorations such as beads takes third place to hide preparation and sewing. Knives for cutting, arrowheads for hunting small and big game, lance points, antler rakes and scapula hoes, scrapers for cleaning, and awls for punching holes in buffalo hides and buckskins were all available for use in the Mandan toolkit for hundreds of years. From ancient times, they were made from stones and bones. The favored stone for tools all over the Northern Plains for thousands of years was Knife River Flint, a light brown, translucent stone that is easy to work into a variety of tools. Flint-knapping was a skill learned early in the earth-lodges and tepees. But as skillfully as they could be worked and as sharp and useful as they were, stone tools were no match for iron tools when it came to durability and strength. Trade metal began replacing stone tools in the 1600s, and its march into the Mandan toolkit was inexorable.

Sometimes the tools of the whites found uses unintended by their manufacturers. A wonderful example is in the fate of the corn mill of Lewis and Clark. On the first night camped by Mitutanka,

October 26, 1804, the Americans hosted a throng of interested Mandan who picked and poked their ways through the remarkable instruments of the alien culture come to their midst. One of the items gaining the most attention was a corn mill. The mill was presented to the Mandan before the Corps of Discovery set out for the Pacific.

Fifteen months after Lewis and Clark went upriver, Alexander Henry the Younger, a manager within the North West Company, came from the Red River to visit the earthlodge villages in the summer of 1806. Henry was, like so many nineteenth century writers, ethnocentric. When he saw that the Mandan had destroyed the corn mill for its metal, he described them as "foolish."[39] He missed the point entirely.

Metal was scarce. Women were not. Alfred Bowers estimated that women outnumbered men almost two to one in the Mandan villages of the middle nineteenth century. Warfare had pared the male population. The ratio was even more extreme if only adults were counted. The relatively abundant women knew how to grind corn using wooden pestles and mortars or grind stones. At a minimum, there was no need to have the corn mill replace women's labor. It may have been, too, that the Mandan found the mill inadequate to the job. They may not have liked the texture or taste of corn milled through the metal as well as stone-ground flour. But metal was precious for other uses. The Mandan cleverly turned the unnecessary corn mill into necessary scrapers and arrow points. The handle even had a use after dismantling. It became a meat tenderizer, a pemmican pounder.

Of all the things the Europeans brought to the New World that found their way to the Missouri, certainly the most world-changing were the gun and the horse. The Mandan say that a visionary dreamed of guns before the people ever saw one. The same was said about horses. The dream about a gun indicated that the Mandan would obtain a weapon that could kill at a great distance.

The first guns likely found their way down from Hudson Bay in the late 1600s. They were not particularly effective at killing at a great distance. But they did make quite a racket and a powerful impression. A man with a bow and arrow might still have a fighting or hunting advantage, particularly in that a man with a bow can fire rapidly and repeatedly. The Mandan trained in exactly that, from childhood. The game of the arrow, as George Catlin called it, was played by boys and men alike. Another advantage of an arrow lay in the ability of an archer to loop the flight so that arrows could rain down on an enemy hidden behind a fortification.

Perhaps the two greatest advantages of the northwest trade guns over bows and arrows were the more or less consistent force of the musket ball and the ability to fire from cover without exposing one-self. With a gun a warrior can unleash a projectile accurately and powerfully from a prone position. And, though the ability of a Plains warrior to fire an arrow clean through a buffalo is legendary, the ability of a musket ball to crash through a rawhide shield was greater than an arrow's chance at a distance.

The first horses might have showed up a little later than the first guns. Most analysts have used the la Verendrye visit to date the advent of the horse among the earthlodge peoples. The analysis is this: He didn't mention horses in his journal of 1738 and he walked home. But in the fall of 1739, the men he left among the Mandan rode horses back to Fort La Reine. In 1742, when his sons returned to the Mandan villages, they found horses and obtained some. Therefore, the horse was first present in Mandan villages around that time.

That may be too simple an argument. First, in the papers leading up to la Verendrye's visit, there is that mention of the Mandan children in Montreal in 1733 telling la Verendrye's nephew, la Jemeraye, when they saw a horse, that they had animals like that back home. Even earlier, according to a painted hide, Baptiste Good's Winter Count, the Dakota stole Mandan and Hidatsa horses in 1728.[40] Then too, if the Mandan just obtained their first horse in 1739 or 1740, would they be in a position to give several up to the French?

Mandan tradition confirms that the nations to their south and west obtained horses before the Mandan did. When la Verendrye visited, he was told that the Panana and Pananis, that is, the Arikara and Pawnee respectively, had horses. Earlier than 1738, the first horses the Mandan saw came with the Cheyenne, brought to one of the villages by the Heart River. The Cheyenne came regularly from the Black Hills to feed their ancient corn habit. One fall, an older mare with a colt was unable to leave the villages, and an elderly Cheyenne woman stayed the winter with the Mandan to care for the horses. The Mandan considered the horses mostly a curiosity.[41]

Regardless of when they first appeared, or the Mandan's lack of enthusiasm for them in the beginning, by the middle of the 1700s and decades before Sheheke's birth, the Mandan were transformed into a horse culture. What formerly were long walks became short rides. Where a dog travois could carry a small amount of meat, a horse travois could carry many times as much. Hunting tactics changed. Bison hunting on foot can be done, obviously, with several methods being very effective, including the buffalo jump, or a version of that where buffalo are stampeded down into a ravine with archers waiting for them above and on the sides. Those group hunts needed to be well-planned and staged. But with trained horses, and skillful riders and archers, many buffalo could be taken much more spontaneously. When buffalo were spotted, a posse could be rounded up in a hurry and dozens of bison would be skinned and butchered before the day was out, even on the shortest days of winter.

The number of horses owned by the Mandan and Hidatsa never seems to have approached the vastness of the herds of the Cheyenne or Crow. The horses of the village nations were reputed to be excellent, but despite their favorable trading position, or actually because of it, the raw number of horses seems to have remained quite small in the five villages. When David Thompson was in the villages in 1797, he declared that the number of horses there was small in relation to the population. He said that a chief with whom he stayed had only three horses and that the entire society had too few horses to satisfy their hunting needs. That great numbers of horses were traded into the villages is a matter of historic record. In 1805 and 1806 alone, in just two recorded negotiations, the Hidatsa obtained 450 horses. With even a laissez-faire breeding non-program, those 450 horses alone should have multiplied into thousands by the time Prince Maximilian of Weid appeared in the villages in 1833. But he counted only 250 to 300 horses in the three Hidatsa villages and 300 more in the two Mandan towns. The most likely explanation is that the villagers were exporting horses as fast or faster than they were importing them.

The white traders from Canada were among the horse shoppers. Certainly the Assiniboine were good customers, too. Though they walked to the Mandan, presumably, with la Verendrye in 1738, a large party of Assiniboine were mounted when Francois and Louis-Joseph, la Verendrye's boys, met up with them in 1743.

One other item the white men brought to the Indians on the Upper Missouri was something borrowed from other Indians far away. The tobacco the traders carried was superior to the tobacco of the great gardeners of the Missouri bottoms. At least the white men generally believed it to be superior. The Mandan and Hidatsa may have just looked at it as a change of pace, another brand with the taste of another climate dried into its leaves.

Whites brought alcohol, of course. Its effects on the Native American population over the four hundred years since the Pilgrims hit Plymouth Rock have been only slightly less hideous than small-pox. In these earliest days of contact on the Plains, though, alcohol problems go almost unmentioned. Maybe the most critical comment on whiskey came from the Arikara who suggested that white traders shouldn't charge for alcohol; rather, they should pay the Indians to drink it, since they must distribute whiskey only to take amusement at the foolish actions of the Indian unlucky enough to drink it. Whiskey is certainly not one of the good things whites brought to the Mandan, but it would have been considered so by some Indians at the time.

Mirrors were quite popular, too. By the 1830s, a little mirror was an essential part of the well-dressed Mandan's outfit. Young Mandan men, Prince Maximilian of Wied said, all carried a small mirror set in a wooden frame swinging from their wrists attached by a piece of rawhide.

Horses, guns, metal tools, and interesting luxury items—some very good things were brought by the whites. That the whites also brought a new and broader cultural view to the Upper Missouri is something that should not be overlooked. As the various Euro-American groups learned about the demographics, economics, and cultural patterns of the Mandan, the Mandan were studying the whites and their physical and cultural multiverse. To a cosmopolitan trading people like the Mandan, new languages, new origin stories, and new cultural traits were all exciting to explore. Yes, for a time, the coming of the whites was a boon to the very old Mandan culture. Throughout Sheheke's childhood, in his formative years all the way through his scheduled graduation from the Foolish Dogs Society, white presence in his world seemed to be an almost unalloyed good thing.

4

Smallpox

Smallpox came to the New World from the Old. It was a highly contagious disease with a high mortality rate. It had swept across Europe in repeated epidemics over millennia, striking at the urban centers of Western civilization. Athens was weakened by smallpox and lost a war to Sparta. Rome saw 2,000 people a day die at the height of a fifteen-year bout with the disease in the second century. It continued to kill Europeans throughout the Middle Ages and into the age of exploration. Smallpox was brought to America by some of its earliest colonists.

Native peoples in America had no previous experience with the disease. Outbreaks of smallpox and other European diseases among East Coast tribes devastated their populations. Intended or not, the diseases brought by the whites cleared the land of its native occupants as surely, and much more quickly, than the frontiersman's ax cleared the primordial eastern forest.

It started with headaches. But by the time they came, the victim had already had smallpox for a week. Then, quickly, came the burning fever, shivers and chills, backache, and a turning stomach. Sleep offered no relief. Terrifying dreams visited then—dreams that continued into a waking delirium. In another week the sick developed rashes, which blistered and broke. Big sores filled with pus scarred victims' faces, hands, and feet. It attacked inside, as well, striking the seventh sacred direction, in the way the Lakota saw things. People began to die from the inside, bleeding under their skin.

After four weeks, if a victim had not died, he or she might start to recover. They would be, most often, scarred for life with marks of the disease, but it would be the only time they would have small-pox. For everyone, smallpox only came once.

On the Great Plains, a school of archeological theory holds that there were repeated incidents of smallpox epidemics in the 1700s, perhaps earlier. Whether or not the Mandan had faced smallpox ear-lier, they had never faced anything like the epidemic of 1781. In fact, the devastating nature of that summer's horror argues against the Mandan having been through earlier waves of smallpox. In 1781, it appears that eighty percent of the Mandan Nation died within a matter of weeks. Seven villages with a population of 10,000 to 15,000 were reduced to two and a half villages totaling maybe 3,000 people.

How Sheheke escaped smallpox is not known. Based on the one drawing of him and the several descriptions, he does not seem to have been marked by the pox. A bit of circumstantial evidence adds to the probability that he never contracted the disease. Clark wrote in his journal about Sheheke's brother giving him a farewell. The chronicler of Sheheke's return to his village also mentions his broth-er providing a feast to Sheheke's entourage in 1809. In Mandan terms, the word "brother" should perhaps not be taken too literally. But if Sheheke did have a brother who survived to adulthood at Mitutanka, then that raises the likelihood that the two didn't con-tract the disease. The most likely way to avoid it is to not come in contact with anyone who has it. Perhaps his family reacted to the epidemic quickly and took or sent the boys off on a hunting trip. Maybe they were away from On-a-Slant when the smallpox came, and were warned not to re-enter the village. A family tradition handed down among one set of Sheheke's descendants holds that, as a young man, maybe fifteen or sixteen years of age, Sheheke traveled all the way to the West Coast and back. It's a reach, but the trip could explain his survival of the pox, if he was on an epic journey when the disease struck On-a-Slant. Or, it could instead help fill in the time gap between the epidemic of 1781 and the settling of Mitutanka. Smallpox could have motivated a young Mandan to go exploring. The years just after the death of the Heart River Phase encouraged unusual behavior. Motivation and opportunity and some circumstantial evidence exists to put Sheheke at the Pacific. But one fact trumps the story. If he had gone to the coast, surely Sheheke would have told William Clark. If he'd been told, Clark would have written about it in his journal.

Whatever the reason Sheheke survived smallpox, his world was forever changed by the epidemic. The power of the Mandan was broken by an unseen enemy.

As the epidemic passed, it left behind not just empty villages, but worse, villages with lodges of death where entire families had passed away, villages with too many dead and too few healthy enough to mourn properly. Some analysts have thought this might explain the significant incidence of burials within On-a-Slant and other Heart River Phase villages.

At Sheheke's On-a-Slant Village, professional archeologists have unearthed eleven cache pit burials. Since they've opened only a couple dozen cache pits under a handful of lodges, that is a very high incidence of burials for a people reputed to have buried their dead on scaffolds in a cemetery beyond their villages' walls. Extrapolated over the entire village area it could mean several hundred burials lay beneath On-a-Slant. Duncan Strong of Columbia University and the Smithsonian Institution found eight of those in a brief 1938 excavation. Strong said that he initially believed that the burials may have been a cultural aberration caused by the overwhelming nature of the epidemic and the inability of the people to keep up their traditions given the rapid pace of death in 1781. But Strong consulted the literature and found that one of Prince Maximilian of Wied's informants, a Mandan named Dipauch, had told Maximilian something on the subject in 1834. Answering the question of why the Mandan didn't bury their dead in the ground like Europeans, Dipauch said that they had formerly done just that and that the Lord of Life wished for them to follow that practice.

The great culture hero told the Mandan, "We come from the ground, and should return to it again." But they abandoned that tradition, Dipauch said, "We have lately begun to lay the bodies of the dead on stages, because we love them and would weep at the sight of them."[42] With that bit of oral tradition as evidence, Strong reconsidered the burials. They were clearly done with care. The deceased had their feet pointed to the southeast, towards the spirit villages some believed they would inhabit after death, their knees were flexed and a few had precious personal items buried with them.

No one has carbon-dated any of the bodies found at On-a-Slant and it would serve little purpose, since the range of possible dates is a two-hundred-year period between two hundred and four hundred years before present. Radiocarbon-dating bones wouldn't be precise enough to place the burials so specifically in time as to indicate whether or not they were from the termination of the village or an earlier era, according to Dennis Toom, a University of North Dakota archeologist working at On-a-Slant from 1999 to 2001.

Burials have been found in other village sites. Double Ditch, more properly known as Yellow Earth Village, has some. There are a considerable number in Scattered Village in the city of Mandan. A 1999 dig under East First Street uncovered thirteen bodies, most of which were identified as women. Care, once again, was shown in their burials. Ochre outlined several bodies, and their orientation was similar to the burials at On-a-Slant.

Whatever the style of burial in use in 1781, the survivors of the epidemic faced a monumental public health hazard. The villages were still virulent, too. Hides had been infected, and smallpox still lurked.

The much-reduced population was insufficient to defend seven villages. If On-a-Slant suffered like the others, its population numbers had dropped to two or three hundred. Of that, as few as fifty might have been healthy adult warriors. The last chief of On-a-Slant, Good Boy, rallied the survivors of his village, including Sheheke and his brother, and people from the four other villages on the west side of the Missouri. Sometime between immediately and four or five years later, they decided that together they'd build a new village at the edge of the Bad Lands where the Little Missouri River enters the big Missouri. The Hidatsa, however, wouldn't allow it.

The Hidatsa Proper were the least sedentary of the various bands of Mandan and Hidatsa. They suffered the least from the smallpox. It was a pattern repeated all over the Great Plains in 1781. While the disease was widespread, the more urban nations, like the Mandan, Hidatsa, and Arikara, suffered much more than did the Lakota, Dakota, Crow, and Cheyenne. This led to a very noticeable shift in the balance of power on the Plains. The nomadic peoples became dominant. The agricultural nations were seriously weakened. Amongst the agricultural people, the ones least tied to the land emerged least damaged by the epidemic.

So when Good Boy led his refugees north, the more numerous and powerful Hidatsa were able to control the conversation. The Mandan could not settle upriver from them, that was reserved hunting territory. But the long friendship of the two peoples and their mutual need for defense brought them to an agreement. The Hidatsa invited the Mandan to live near them, just a few miles downriver from the mouth of the Knife River. The new village of Mitutanka was established as the southern frontier city of the Knife River village complex. It provided some protection for Metaharta, a city with both Awatixa and Mandan families, and Mahawha, the last city of the plucky but weakened Wattasoons.

South was where the most danger lay. The Arikara and the Mandan had been fighting for four hundred years or more, and that conflict was not forgotten just because they had both been weakened by smallpox. The Lakota and Cheyenne most often came from the south, too. Mitutanka would be the closest city in the five-village metropolitan area to receive their attentions.

Eventually, sometime before 1797, Nuptadi Village appeared on the east bank of the Missouri, just north of Mitutanka. The Mandan from Yellow Earth Village and the Larson site moved there after trying and failing to make things work at Yellow Earth. Pressure from the Sioux helped bring about the consolidation of the last Mandans with the four villages already at the Knife River.

Good Boy was chief of Mitutanka for nine years. He died between 1790 and 1795. Sometime after that, Sheheke became a chief at Mitutanka. He had to navigate complex political waters, attempting to maintain national independence for his people when they were at least codependent with the Hidatsa in facing attacks from their hostile neighbors. Smallpox had changed everything. It had changed everything for the worse.

5

Before Lewis and Clark

The first European, or more specifically, the first Euro-Canadian visitor to the Missouri River in what is now North Dakota is also the most famous white visitor before Lewis and Clark. But he was far from the only one. From the time of la Verendrye's trip to the Missouri in 1738, to the October day in 1804 when Lewis and Clark rowed into sight, the villages of the Mandan and Hidatsa were seldom without white traders.

Pierre Gaultier de Varennes, la Sieur de la Verendrye, was born in 1685 in Three Rivers, Quebec. Though he was born the son and the grandson of successive governors of Three Rivers, Pierre grew up without wealth or a father, as Governor Rene Gaultier died when Pierre was only four years old. Pierre, la Verendrye, as he's remembered to history, became a soldier, a cadet in the colonial regulars, when he was just eleven. He fought for France in the New World and the Old. He was with a French and Indian unit that attacked Deerfield, Massachusetts, in 1704. He fought in Europe, became a lieutenant after suffering serious wounds, and was captured by the Spanish at the Battle of Malplaquet.[43]

Being a lieutenant in the French army was an expensive proposition. Costly social obligations went along with the rank—more than a lieutenant's pay would allow. Not being independently wealthy, la Verendrye's promotion forced his retirement from the military.

He went home to Three Rivers at age twenty-six and married the local French girl to whom he had been engaged before leaving for Europe. Marie-Anne had a fair dowry and the couple had six children and eked out a living for fifteen years on a little farm on the Ile aux Vaches. Adding to the couple's income was la Verendrye's interest in a fur trade post founded by his father. He was destined to become much more involved in the fur trade.

Crashing out of his mid-life crisis, la Verendrye was welcomed into a new fur trade business by his brother. It was a successful attempt to expand the territory of French trading into the Canadian interior, the area north of Lake Superior. In 1728, his brother went off to war and left la Verendrye commander-in-chief of a huge area of Canada's western frontier. It was then that an idea poured in and began to percolate in his mind. He wanted to find the route to the Western Sea.

This was not a unique personal obsession. It was actually an international pastime for centuries, but one that was particularly popular with the French in the 1700s. There was, the French hoped, a bay or inland sea stretching toward the Pacific somewhere just beyond their farthest penetration of the North American continent. A western river might flow to it.

At his post on the Nipigon River, la Verendrye questioned visiting Indians about the land to the west and, particularly, the water to the west. The Cree and the Assiniboine told him many things, some of which were true. He heard about interesting people who lived on a major river of the West. They were the Mandan and Hidatsa, seen as one people by all chroniclers until 1797. They were called by a variety of names, but la Verendrye, for reasons unknown, settled on the *Mantannes*. A Mandan slave, a man who had been captured by the Cree and served the elderly chief Vieux Crapaud, told la Verendrye that the Mandan were a very prosperous people. He said their country was heavily populated and their villages extended for leagues into the plains beyond the banks of the Missouri. They were a people who did not have canoes and only precious little wood. They burned dried dung for fuel in its stead. The gardens of

Mandan women were very productive, he told la Verendrye, and the people had abundant supplies of game and fruit to vary their diets.

The Cree, recognizing a language stock when they heard it, told la Verendrye that they called those Indians, *Ouachipouennes*, or "the Sioux who go underground." The Ouachipouennes had eight villages, with fields of Indian corn, melons, pumpkins, and beans. They lived like the French, in buildings of wood and earth. The Ouachipouennes were the same height as other Indians, the Cree told la Verendrye, but some had red hair, some blonde, and some black. Other stories came from the Assiniboine. They told him about bearded farmers who lived along the river of the West. Their descriptions may have been of Spanish settlers in the Southwest or the Southern Plains, but to la Verendrye they were the same people the Cree called Ouachipouennes. All the stories fueled his imagination. La Verendrye decided to visit these people and their river to gain information about the route to the Western Sea.

An Indian named Auchagah created a birchbark map for la Verendrye that showed Lake Winnipeg with the Red River running into it and the Nelson River running north out of it to Hudson Bay. The map fancifully also showed a large river flowing west out of the lake. La Verendrye took that map back to Quebec and showed it to the Governor of New France, General Beauharnois. He asked the Governor for help organizing a western exploration. Beauharnois was agreeable and asked the French crown for sanction and financial assistance. The first was no problem. La Verendrye was encouraged to pursue his dream. Financing, though, was a problem. No money was forthcoming, but la Verendrye did get a negotiable currency; he was given a three-year trading monopoly on goods from the new territory. He parlayed his royal award into cash through the backing of the trading houses of Montreal and Quebec.

In 1738, la Verendrye was ready. Now fifty-three years of age, the old veteran set out on foot to explore the unknown West. From his own Fort Rouge, modern-day Winnipeg, he walked to the Missouri River in the late fall of 1738, stopping briefly to establish Fort La Reine along the old trade route that passed Portage la Prairie. The trip was lengthened considerably by his guides, Assiniboine Indians.

Before Lewis and Clark

When he started out from Fort La Reine in early October, la Verendrye had a party of twenty-five Frenchmen and twenty-five Assiniboine guides. The Assiniboine led him in a zigzag across the Northern Plains, visiting various camps of their nation. The exploration gained a lot of hangers-on. By the time they left the last Assiniboine camp and finally headed directly for the Mantannes villages, there were six hundred Indians in the party.

As would happen sixty-six years later with Lewis and Clark, a small group of Mantannes came out to greet la Verendrye when he was still a day away from their village. A flurry of trading took place and la Verendrye found the Mantannes to be "cunning traders, cheating the Assiniboines of all they may possess, such as muskets, powder, balls, kettles, axes, knives and awls." Years of contact with native peoples hadn't shaken his ethnocentrism. He saw the European goods flowing into Mandan or Hidatsa hands and saw it as a one-sided deal. What la Verendrye missed, no doubt, was that the products of the Missouri River villagers had their own appeal. He himself noted that the Mantannes "dressed leather better than any of the other nations, and work in furs and feathers very tastefully, which the Assiniboines are not capable of doing." The Assiniboine didn't grow corn, either, but they liked to eat it. The trading la Verendrye saw was not cheating, it was an exchange that benefitted both parties. It wouldn't have happened otherwise.

Aghast at the huge throng, which would place a strain on their traditional hospitality, the Mantannes told their visitors that their mutual enemy, the Sioux, were on the warpath and in the area. They thanked the Assiniboine for delivering their white friends and their European goods safely. Now, they could and should leave. The Assiniboine seemed to consider that good advice, but were forcefully lectured by an old warrior. They had signed on to deliver their white friend to the Mantannes village, he declared, and it was a matter of honor that they see it through. The younger men, their courage challenged, had to agree. Consequently, the parade was still on. Some of the Assiniboine did split off, some of the warriors escorting most of the women, children, and elders back to their home country.

On the third day of December, the month of the Little Cold, in 1738, la Verendrye was carried into the nearest village. It was the smallest of all the Mantannes' villages and was the only one not located on the banks of the Missouri. It was less than half a day's walk away from the river.[44] It had 130 earthlodges and a protective ditch surrounding it. The ditch was fifteen feet deep and eighteen feet across. The village sat on a height of prairie, according to la Verendrye.

La Verendrye's eyewitness account of his eight days amongst the Mantannes is the earliest recorded. At first he was disappointed in the Mantannes, as they appeared to him to be as Indian in their physical traits and material culture as were the Assiniboine, but subsequently he declared the people he found to be somewhat as advertised.

> This nation is mixed white and black. The
> women are fairly good looking, especially the light
> colored ones, many of them have blond or fair hair.
> Both the men and the women of this tribe are very
> industrious. Their lodges are large and spacious, sepa-
> rated into several apartments by broad planks.
> Nothing is left lying about; for all their belongings
> are kept in large bags which are hung on posts. Their
> beds are made like tombs surrounded by skins. All
> go to bed naked, men and women. These men are
> always naked and for covering they use buffalo
> robes. Most of the women go naked like the men,
> with this difference, that they wear a loin cloth
> about a hand breadth wide and a span long, sewed
> to a girdle in front. All the women have this kind of
> protection, even those who wear petticoats, so that
> they suffer no embarrassment when they sit down
> as is the case with other Indian women. Several of
> them wear a kind of jacket of very soft roe deer skin
> [pronghorn antelope]. This species of deer is abun-
> dant and is very small. . . . They are fond of tatooing,

but never more than half of the body is tatooed,
both of men and women. They make wicker work
very neatly, flat and in baskets. They make use of
earthen pots, which they use like many other nations
for cooking their food. They are for the most part
great eaters; are eager for feasts. They brought me
every day more than twenty dishes of wheat, beans
and pumpkins, all cooked. . . . The men are stout and
tall, generally very active, fairly good looking, with a
good physiognomy and very affable. The women
have not the Indian physiognomy. The men indulge
in a sort of ball play on the squares and ramparts.[45]

La Verendrye learned painfully little more through conversation
with the Mantannes. The language barrier was too difficult. La
Verendrye had made plans to overcome the barrier, but they went
awry. The language chain was to go from la Verendrye's French to
his son's French and Cree, to an Assiniboine who spoke Cree, to the
Mantannes, some of whom spoke Assiniboine. When the Assiniboine
split up, one of the women who went home was a young woman
with whom the Cree-to-Assiniboine translator had fallen in love.
He went after her. The chain of communication was broken.

When la Verendrye, chilled and sick, walked back to Fort La
Reine, he left behind two men, placed in separate villages to facilitate their learning of the language. One of those may have been
Pierre la Chappelle who wrote a book, *Contes et Voyages*, published
in Paris in 1774, which contained information about his time with
the Mandan. He had a tough time learning much of the language,
but he was a more careful student of their love rites, which he called
"a remarkable combination of primitive, lascivious ceremonies and a
romantic code of behaviour that had a flavor of the troubadours."[46]
He described a musical instrument, a type of harp, apparently used
only ceremonially. La Chappelle said that the erotic rites the
Mandan practiced attracted many visitors from among the European
traders.

The two language students rode back to Fort La Reine in

September of 1739.[47] It's likely that they were quickly replaced by other representatives of the French. There were at least three different Frenchmen among the Mandan in those earliest years of contact. Two of la Verendrye's sons, Francois, la Chevalier, and Louis-Joseph returned to the Missouri in 1742, along with two Mandan-speaking Frenchmen. Neither of those translators was named la Chappelle, who had problems learning the language anyway. There was continued contact with the Mandan in 1740–42, producing at least one more Mandan speaker than the one who came out of the 1738 expedition. The search for the Western Sea continued, with the sons re-visiting the people they had met four years earlier and then extending their range to the south and west. They rode, instead of walked, from the Mantannes that time, as they investigated the high plains to the foothills of the Big Horns. They left lead plates marking their passage above the Missouri near what became Pierre, South Dakota. They were among the Mandan, or Hidatsa, for two months in the spring of 1742 and then again for a similar length of time in the spring of 1744.

There isn't much information available about white contact with the Mandan over the next four decades. That trade continued is a certainty. That white visitors were there, at times, is known. It's likely that resident traders were there throughout the period, but record-keeping was lax and journals, if kept, haven't been found. It's unfortunate there isn't more known, because when journalists do take up the quill in the 1790s, the Mandan and Hidatsa are shadows of their former selves. The Mandan are refugees. Literate men, or at least men from a literate culture, saw the Mandan in their Golden Age, but only the few paragraphs by la Verendrye exist to tell about them, if in fact he visited a Mandan village and not one of the Hidatsa.

The French gave up most of their territorial claims in North America in 1762, just before surrendering to the English in the Treaty of Paris, 1763, ending what Americans know as the French and Indian War. They secretly ceded Louisiana to the Spanish, rather than allow it to be taken by the British. Thereafter, while many of the fur traders and engagees were of French descent, they were no longer working for French companies or the French crown, they were working either for English companies, or for themselves.

A brisk competition for a not very profitable trade developed over time. Distracted by their protracted war for the continent, French and British traders made infrequent visits to the Missouri until the 1770s. Then the pace picked up.

A fur trader named Mackintosh was among the Mandan on Christmas Day, 1773, but all that history records is a single line, quoted by Henry Rowe Schoolcraft, that the Mandan at that time had nine villages, a number that contradicts what Sheheke later told Lewis and Clark. Sheheke said there were seven villages when he lived at On-a-Slant. Mackintosh and Sheheke were probably both right, but referring to different things. While it is possible that two villages were abandoned between 1773 and 1781, that is not the most likely reason for the disparity in counting. It was probably a matter of definition. Which villages did each man count as Mandan? In adding two to Sheheke's count, Mackintosh could have easily been adding two villages of the Awatixa Hidatsa, so close to the Mandan that they were sometimes referred to as the Northern Mandan.

A trader named Menard was resident among the Mandan from about 1778 to 1804. The time of his arrival among the Mandan has forever been a source of speculation. Different chroniclers of his acquaintance have him arriving between 1765 and 1788, with the citations including his first coming among the Mandan forty years before 1805,[48] and sixteen years before either 1792 or 1804.[49] He did not leave any personal account of his time, though he appears in others' reports, each of them differing in reference to his arrival on the Missouri. He may, or may not, have been among the villagers when the epidemic of 1781 hit. It is agreed, though, that Menard spent a long time living with the Missouri River villagers and he was the first white man to see the Yellowstone River. He claimed to have traveled 150 leagues up it, a distance of perhaps 450 miles, taking him to its source in the Rocky Mountains at Yellowstone Lake. Menard, a free trader sometimes associated with the North West Company, had a Mandan woman, "fair and graceful for his wife," according to geographer David Thompson. They lived in a village reported to have housed thirty-seven Mandan families and fifteen Awatixi Hidatsa lodges. They had no children. Menard himself was clever and good-looking. According to Thompson, Menard "was an intelligent man, but completely a Frenchman, brave, gay and boastful." Menard was killed by the Assiniboine in September 1804, just prior to the arrival of Lewis and Clark. The explorers' information about the decades before their visit and the path ahead of them would have been much more complete had Menard lived.

Menard qualifies as a "free trader." He sometimes worked for others as a contractor, but he maintained an independence that allowed him to stay with his wife in the Mandan villages, set out for the Rockies, and trade goods or not on his own schedule. The free traders, and their Mandan and Hidatsa trading partners, benefited from a long-standing competition between major fur trading companies.

The Hudson's Bay Company's influence was felt in the interior as early as the 1600s. But the Company of Adventurers just took what flowed to them at their post called York Factory at the end of the basin taking in the Red, the Souris and the Assiniboine Rivers. They held court on Hudson Bay for more than a hundred years before finally opening a fort on the Assiniboine River in 1793. Then they came because they were invited to support the previously losing side in a competition between an independent trader and the North West Company, founded by Montreal businessmen and fueled by the French, Scotch, and Metis voyageurs and engagees plying the old la Verendrye canoe trail leading from the lakes and rivers of Manitoba, Saskatchewan, and North Dakota to the ocean-going ports on the St. Lawrence River. The North West Company set up forts on the Assiniboine River in 1780.

Also in 1780, in November, a North West Company partner, Donald Mackay, with four voyageurs set off to visit the Mandan villages. Their Cree guide demanded a raise in his contracted fee, once he had them out on the, for some, too trackless prairie. The demand was rejected, and the guide disappeared. The Nor'westers were lost. They were in trouble, with a Northern Plains winter coming on. Temperatures can and do drop to forty below, the only number that's exactly as frigid in centigrade as in Fahrenheit. Wind chill temperatures drop to eighty or even one hundred below zero in blinding blizzards. Mackay hunkered down somewhere southeast of the Turtle Mountains. Found in mid-March by some local Assiniboine who were impressed with their survival skills, Mackay's party was rescued and guided to the Hidatsa villages along the Knife. They were extremely popular there, Mackay recounted, being hosted to an elaborate reception with feasting and gifts. It was his presumption that the welcome was intense because traders were lately infrequent.

The smallpox epidemic of 1781 interfered with trade resuming and put in motion armed battles along the Assiniboine River, temporarily driving white traders back to the Red River. The villages reshuffled, the survivors occupying a cluster of five towns near the mouth of the Knife.

In 1783, the North West Company was back. They built Pine Fort along the Assiniboine near the Portage la Prairie, and built Fort Esperance on the Qu'Appelle River in modern-day Saskatchewan. It was from the latter that James Mackay, a literate Scotsman, visited the Missouri in 1787. He walked down from Fort Esperance in the middle of winter. It was a seventeen-day journey that would have taken ten, he figured, in another season. This Mackay had come to the British possessions in North America at age seventeen in the turbulent year of 1776. Coming west, he became engaged in the fur trade. But his interest turned to the search for the legendary northwest passage.[50] It was clear by his time that no convenient all-water route from Atlantic to Pacific existed between the Arctic and Tierra del Fuego, but whatever the most convenient land and water route might be was still a hotly sought commodity. His visit to the Mandan helped him forge an understanding of the Upper Missouri region and a possible route to the Western Sea.

In 1792, Jean D'eglise came to the Mandan. Given a license by Spain to hunt in the Missouri country, he found it possible to slip his pirogue past nomadic hunting parties and the many villages of sedentary agricultural Indians along the Missouri. Through the territory of the Lakota and past the Arikara, often traveling at night and always as unobtrusively and nonthreateningly as possible, he reached the Knife River region. D'eglise brought greetings from the Spanish king, Charles IV, yet another great father of the whites. He brought few things to trade, however. When he ran out of goods, he left, promising to return with more supplies.

It never happened. The Arikara jealously guarded their trading relationship with St. Louis. The next Spanish trading party was stopped when it tried to ascend with pirogues filled with goods to trade with the Mandan.

In the early 1790s, the Mandan trade in European goods still came exclusively from the north. By 1793, there were competing posts on the Assiniboine River, strategically located at the mouth of the Souris River. That was the year Donald Mackay, the same former North West Company man who visited the Hidatsa in the spring of 1781, built Brandon House for the Hudson's Bay Company. Mackay had severed ties with the North West Company and set out to try his hand as a free trader on the Qu'Appelle. After he'd gone independent, the Nor'westers roughed him up and squashed his business in Saskatchewan in 1785–87. Mackay wanted to get even. He appealed for financial support and some muscle from the Hudson's Bay Company. They made the move to the Assiniboine and Souris, some miles west and upriver from Pine Fort, the North West Company post formerly receiving the Souris trade.

Though they are on opposite sides of a continental divide, the walk from the Souris to the Missouri is an easy jaunt of forty miles. Easy in that there are no elevation problems; there often were problems, though, with enormous herds of buffalo, prairie fires, blizzards, and seasonal drought sometimes compounded by a thorough lack of local information. But traffic made the crossing, from both directions.

Trade flowed along the Souris River loop.[51] The placement of two competing forts (Brandon House and an independent post) at the mouth of the Souris meant the rapid abandonment of Pine Fort around 1794. Though it had long served the Mandan trade, it wasn't without troubles even before the Hudson's Bay folks moved in. The trade depended on providing credit to independent fur traders who

Before Lewis and Clark

took skins from the posts with the condition that they would pay for them upon their return. The credit situation didn't last long. The country was too big and too many men took the skins on credit and deserted to the Illinois country and other places on the Mississippi. One who deserted to the Lower Missouri country was James Mackay, though there has been no allegation that he owed anything to his former employers. He was destined to play an important role for his new bosses, the Spanish. James Mackay switched countries in 1793, going to work for the Spanish-chartered Missouri Company. By 1795, he was named manager of the Missouri Company's affairs on the Upper Missouri. He wasted no time in renewing his quest to find a way from the Missouri to the Pacific.

Mackay set out to visit the Mandan in 1795, taking a complement of thirty-three engagees in four pirogues loaded with goods. One pirogue's treats were to buy the expedition's way past any Lakota or Dakota people they might meet. One was to trade with the Arikara. One was destined for the Mandan and one was intended to aid in reaching the source of the Missouri, crossing the Rocky Mountains and proceeding to the ocean beyond.

Mackay expected his mission to take as long as six years, not because the goal was so distant, but because the mission was to proceed in careful stages, with diplomatic goals to accomplish along the way. Time would be taken to construct forts at strategic locations on the route. The expedition's mission statement was "to open commerce with those distant and Unknown Nations in the upper parts of the Missouri and to discover all the unknown parts of his Catholic Majesty's Dominions through that continent as far as the Pacific Ocean."[52]

The trip was a disaster in terms of achieving its ambitious goals. Leaving St. Louis in the late summer of 1795, Mackay made slow progress upriver. With winter coming on, he established Fort Charles near the Omaha Indians. Mackay tried to deflect their craving for his limited and targeted goods by promising regular visits from the traders at St. Louis. He sent his lieutenant, John Evans, overland to reach the Arikara, presumably to grease the skids for the larger

Spanish expedition coming the following spring. Evans set out, but near the White River his group was spooked by a Lakota hunting party and he beat a hasty retreat back to Mackay at Fort Charles.

On January 28, 1796, Evans received a much more ambitious commission from MacKay. Evans was to ascend the Missouri, perhaps to the Mandan, but his real mission only started there. He was given a secret mission to cross the Rockies and reach the Pacific Ocean. He was instructed that if he learned of a shortcut to the Yellowstone that avoided the Mandan villages, he was to take it. MacKay told Evans to travel inconspicuously. He was to camp in valleys and not make a fire,

> without a true need, and you will avoid having
> the smoke seen from afar. . . . You will not camp too
> early and will always leave before day-break; you will
> always be on guard against ambushes and will always
> have your arms in good condition; changing the tin-
> der evening and morning, and you will never sepa-
> rate them from you or place them in the hands of
> the savages. . . . Appear always on guard and never be
> fearful or timid, for the savages are not generally
> bold, but will act in a manner to make you afraid
> of them.

MacKay urged him to be on the lookout for a one-horned animal in the Rockies. Evans was to bring back "alive if possible, [animals] unknown to us." Portages were to be marked for later expeditions and Evans was to leave the marks of King Charles IV and the Missouri Company along with his date of passage at various points. That was a practice he was to suspend when he crossed the Rockies, because he might there run into a Russian settlement with a counter-claim to the region. So far from home and without support, he was not to unnecessarily annoy the Russians and thereby imperil his mission.

MacKay's trusted lieutenant, however, had mixed motivations. MacKay believed that Evans shared his excitement at the quest for the source of the Missouri and a route to the Pacific. MacKay should have checked Evans' résumé. Evans was more interested in the quest for lost Welshmen than a quest for the route to the Pacific.

John Evans came to America in 1792 from his native Wales. Stirred by Welsh legends of a Prince Madoc who supposedly led a twelfth-century voyage to colonize the Western Hemisphere, Evans came to America searching for Madoc's descendants. Like so many before him, he thought he might find the Welsh on the Upper Missouri in the villages of the Mandan. He found his way to St. Louis and went to work for a man who had been among the Mandan and who promised to go to them again, if only as a way station in a larger mission. So, when given the chance, Evans did not avoid the Mandan, but paddled into their midst on September 23, 1796.

Evans probably stopped with his crew where Lewis and Clark would eight years later, in the bottoms alongside some harvested corn fields just east of Mitutanka. His boat was instantly greeted by dozens of youngsters and some curious adults, judging by the consistent behavior of the Mandan toward strangers. They would have been waiting for him. Evans was almost certainly observed for several hours, as his pirogue fought a strong current, and probably the prevailing and reliable northwest wind, before making the big bend of the Missouri east of the Mandan village.

Sheheke, thirty years old and either a chief or a man on that career path, would have been one of those who parlayed with Evans. The meeting could not have been very productive, however. Evans spoke English and undoubtedly tried a little Welsh without success. Some of his engagees spoke Spanish, and others French, but none knew Mandan. Hospitality has a language of its own, however, and tradition meant that Evans was made aware that he was welcome as a guest in the Mandan village.

After food and tobacco, Evans may have asked if there were any white men among the Mandan who might aid in translation. Having partnered with James MacKay, who knew first-hand about Canadian traders in the villages, it would have come as no big surprise to learn that Rene Jessaume, a Frenchman who spoke excellent Mandan, had a Mandan wife and a little fur trading fort to the north of Mitutanka. Jessaume had come to the Upper Missouri villages in 1794. Another of the many Frenchman in English Canada, Jessaume established a post near the Mandan and began a long association with the earthlodge peoples. He married a Mandan woman, according to some accounts, though she was also referred to as a resident of the Hidatsa village of Metaharta. She could have been both Mandan and from Metaharta. There were actually more Mandan lodges there than Awatixa Hidatsa. It is most likely she actually was Mandan, since Jessaume's later usefulness to Lewis and Clark was as an interpreter for the Mandan chief, Sheheke. The Jessaumes had children together, at least one boy and girl. Rene Jessaume remained among the Mandan at least twenty years. Evans learned that Jessuame was on a visit to the north when he arrived. Evans and his men took advantage of Jessaume's absence, seized the almost-empty post and raised the Spanish flag over it.

Ensconced in his captured fort, Evans gave some presents to Mandan and Hidatsa chiefs who came to visit, and he proclaimed to them that they had a new great father, Charles IV, who would see to their needs henceforth. They would need to trade with the Hudson's Bay Company, the North West Company, the XY Company, or any others from British Canada no longer. This last item didn't sit well with the earthlodge peoples, particularly the Hidatsa Proper who were closely aligned with the Canadians. But it was easy to ignore Evans' edict in the interest of polite commerce.

Evans sent a note north, a letter from James MacKay, informing MacKay's former employers that they were no longer welcome along the Missouri. It was Spanish territory and they could no longer illegally engage in trade there. On October 8, Cuthbert Grant replied from his homebase at River Tremblante in Canada and accepted, apparently with tongue firmly in cheek, the declaration of the Spanish-chartered Missouri Company.

Grant told Evans that he was willing "to withdraw what little property the N. W. Co. has their, indeed it has been my wish for some time past as we have lost a good deal of money by Mr. Gousseaume whom we have employed in that business."

Other communications with the north made clear the Spanish intentions. Evans was asked in a letter from James Sutherland at Brandon House, dated November 23, 1796, if the prohibition against Canadians extended to the men of the Hudson's Bay Company.

> Your written decleration . . . has come into our hands, forbidding all British Subjects from Trading at the Missurie, this may effect the Traders from Canada, but very little those from Hudsons Bay — I should be glad however to know if we may be permitted on any future occasion to visit the Mandals and Trade Horses, Indian corn and Buffalo robes which articles we supose to be unconnected with the Furt Trade and consiquently expect you will have no objections to . . . [53]

Oh, but Evans did object. And he ran a bluff.

> As to your requist concerning admission to Trade Horses, Indian Corn and Buffalo Robes, it is not in my power to answer you on that head; But I have reason to believe the latter will not be permitted as it is the staple Trade of this Countrie, but however you will be properly inform'd after the arrival of the Agent General and Lieut. Mooroch at this Post . . . [54]

There was no agent or any military force coming.

When Evans ran out of goods and his bluffs lost credibility, he was in trouble. In late February, he found a party from Canada at his doorstep with four sleds loaded with goods. They were met by three hundred Indians who carried the sleds on their shoulders into a village, showing their affection for the British trade. The natives were unhappy when Evans insinuated himself into the situation as a middleman, thereby preserving the fiction that he was preventing British trade with the earthlodge people, since the British were trading with

Evans and Evans was trading with the Hidatsa, but with his status in the middle, he also jacked up the price.

In mid-March, the moon of Sore Eyes, Rene Jessaume returned. He brought presents for the Mandan and Hidatsa leading men, hoping to enlist their support. Evans later reported to his superiors that Jessaume attempted to incite the Mandan to murder, suggesting that they enter the fur post as friends and then fall upon Evans and kill him.

Evans also told his bosses that Jessaume, failing in his conspiracy due to the loyalty and protection certain Mandan men gave to Evans, decided to take matters into his own hands. Jessaume tried to shoot Evans, who was warned in the nick of time by one of his translators. But whatever native support or concern he may have gathered melted with the spring weather. Evans' disappointment at finding that the Mandan had no traditions of descent from Welshmen was matched by Mandan disappointment with Evans' paltry supply of trade goods. By early April, it was clear to all that Evans had overplayed his hand and outstayed his welcome. He was forcefully encouraged to leave. The Canadians returned.

David Thompson came to the Mandan and Hidatsa in 1797. A careful geographer, Thompson was the first writer to draw a distinction between the Mandan and Hidatsa. The term Mandan, or Mantannes, or Mandanes, had been used to describe all the villages of Mandan and Hidatsa from la Verendrye to Evans. Even a decade after Thompson, an observant student of the cultures like Charles Mackenzie slips back and forth between the terms. A Hidatsa is sometimes a Hidatsa, and a Mandan is always a Mandan, but a Hidatsa could also be a Mandan, in the broader context of the five villages.

The North West Company kept up its interest in the Missouri trade, sending parties there annually in the first part of the 1800s. During the first years of the nineteenth century, a free trader named Jean Baptiste LaFrance was engaged in the Missouri trade.[55] He was not literate, so he left no journal or letters of his experience. LaFrance was hired as a guide, interpreter, and clerk to lead a North West Company expedition to the Missouri in the fall of 1804.

Before Lewis and Clark

Charles Mackenzie was selected as an assistant to chronicle the trading party. Through the coincidence of Mackenzie's presence on the Missouri at the same time as the journal-keeping Lewis and Clark Expedition, historians have a variety of viewpoints of this critical moment in Northern Plains culture, somewhat making up for the lack of chroniclers in the previous century. Mackenzie was there for parts of 1804, 1805, and 1806, as were the Americans. The Nor'westers party, including Mackenzie, LaFrance, and Francois Antoine LaRocque, left Fort La Souris on November 18, 1804, unaware that Americans had already taken up residence at the Knife River villages.

6

"If We Eat, You Shall Eat"

In the month of the Fall of Leaves, on October 24, 1804, twenty-five men in a Mandan hunting party waited on a large island near the old and abandoned Yellow Earth Village while a flotilla from the young United States of America made its way up the Missouri. The two nations would meet for the first time on that island. The meeting was entirely friendly, as have been the relations between the United States and the Mandan Nation forever after.

It seems certain that the Mandan knew the Americans were coming and dispatched a party of warriors to greet them. The Mandan, being pretty astute and worldly diplomats, used a hunting camp, complete with tepees and wives carefully left a mile away upriver, to avoid alarming their guests and to cloak their concern about the armed party of white men bringing a unique boat up the Missouri River. Lewis and Clark made an average of eleven water miles a day for the week after they passed the Cannonball River. For a whole week, in October, the driest month of the year in North Dakota, and usually one of the best for travel because there are no mosquitoes, it would be inconceivable that the unusual and hardly inconspicuous Northwest Corps of Discovery would go undiscovered. They were in the hunting country of the Mandan, and it was hunting season. Certainly they would have been noticed sometime during the three days after they passed On-a-Slant's ruins on October 20.

Since a man on a horse could cover the distance from the ruins of the On-a-Slant Village to the Knife River in a hard day's ride, it is very likely that the village of Mitutanka had time to hold council over the appearance of the Americans, who were carrying the Arikara chief *Arketarnawhar Was-to-ne*, Is-a-Whippoorwill,[56] with them. If he was within reach of the village, Sheheke would have been central to the discussions.

Sheheke was the civil chief, the counterpart to the war chief of the Mandan village. Both positions were bestowed by the village council of bundle owners. Neither title was hereditary, though sons of chiefs often rose to those positions.[57] A war chief was chosen for obvious reasons. He showed leadership skills, courage, skill in combat, and an ability to lead a war party to success without getting his men killed. George Custer would not have been elected as a Mandan war chief. He had remarkable success in battle before his one spectacular defeat, but even at his Civil War best, he lost too many soldiers to be a Mandan kind of leader. The United States always had another man to replace a casualty, the Mandan Nation did not.

A civil chief was chosen for other reasons. Sheheke was chosen for his compassion, his concern for the less fortunate, his generosity, and his faithful adherence to the traditions of his people. The civil chief was expected to have the interests of the people at heart. He was the one, according to Alfred Bowers, "who was thoughtful of others, gave frequent feasts, was popular with the tribes coming to the village to trade, and was able to settle little quarrels within the village or with visiting tribes."[58] Both chiefs needed to be persuasive speakers, since the only style of leadership likely to succeed with the Mandan was oratorical. That skill would necessarily be more finally honed among the ranks of civil chiefs. Sheheke could talk.

The two-chief system is what Alfred Bowers says the Mandan had. His interviews with elders, beginning in the 1920s, provided his information. Clearly, Lewis and Clark did not see the same kind of structure, identifying several chiefs in every village. They named a first and second chief, probably by observation, and then also listed a number of other chiefs. In Mitutanka, Clark identified Sheheke as the "1st Chief" and the "Main Chief." He called Little Raven, whose name was more likely Little Crow, the second chief. He also named Big Man and Coal as "two of their Grand Chiefs." Actually, Clark might have been on to something. The theoretical ideal of the two-chief system may have been disrupted in the early nineteenth century. The merger of five villages into one meant the submersion of independent villages one into the other. There may have been a surplus of chiefs and sons of chiefs with followings. There may have been numerous chiefs in the village, though Coal and Big Man are hardly representative of the merger theory. They have more to do with the broad-mindedness of the Mandan, and their severe lack of manpower. Coal, *Sho-ta-har ro-ra*, was an adopted Arikara and Big Man, *Oh-he-nar*, an adopted Cheyenne. Lewis and Clark were probably right about the numerous chiefs, and they were certainly right about who the first one was, Sheheke. His voice mattered in the village councils.

The council on the appearance of the Lewis and Clark Expedition would have reviewed the facts. This was the largest party of white men ever to visit their region. It was by far larger than any that had come from the south. As James Ronda has pointed out, there was no mistaking that this was a heavily armed group. "Trading parties always carried guns but no Indian could have confused this traveling infantry company for a trader' brigade. Weapons of all shapes and sizes—small cannons, pistols, rifles, muskets and knives—were displayed for all to see."[59]

One of the considerations in the village discussion was John Evans. He had been unceremoniously evicted and the party coming could be his people, perhaps out to punish the villages for their treatment of Evans, or to once again try to throw the Canadian traders out of the Mandan villages. Neither of those were happy prospects. Evans had thrown around high-flying talk about Lieutenant Mooroch and a military force coming to solidify the Spanish position on the Upper Missouri. The Mandan and Hidatsa had branded him a liar when no relief column ever arrived. But there were men in uniform among this new white party and they were well-enough equipped to cause a great deal of trouble, if that was their intent.

A second discussion revolved around the Arikara chief. The two Indian nations had a long history, to say the least, of armed conflict. Recently, the Arikara were less eager to maintain hostile relations than they had been in previous centuries. The Arikara felt pressure from their neighbors, the nomadic Lakota, in a couple of ways. They were, on occasion, a bad influence. Lakota raiding parties sometimes included Arikara warriors along for the ride and plunder. The Arikara were also subject to bullying and violence from Sioux sources. Faced with the united front of the Hidatsa and Mandan, a large element of the Arikara population was not interested in war just then. They were even considering, around this time, abandoning their villages at the Grand River and moving north to join forces with the other two earthlodge peoples.

On that particular October day in 1804, the state of diplomatic affairs between the Arikara and the Mandan was unsettled by an individual kidnapping that had taken place during the summer. A married woman had, in late July, either been kidnapped or had eloped with another man. Her father's horse was killed by her husband's father in retribution for his daughter running off with her kidnapper. General war threatened to break out. Violence escalated from horses to people, with a man and woman being killed and growing forces armed and arrayed. Three days of councils led to a temporary truce, but things had remained tense in the months since. A month after the council the Arikara sent a message of peace to the Mandan. The message was garbled, though, by continuing violence stirred up by bands unhappy with the prospects of an earthlodge village alliance. Now, here came an Arikara chief with a heavily armed party of white men.

How these white men had passed the Lakota interested the Mandan. The Sioux must have allowed them passage. No party of forty-six men, no matter how well-armed, could either sneak or fight its way through the thousands of Lakota and Dakota warriors claiming territory on both sides of the Missouri. These men didn't look like they had been fighting. No one in sight appeared to be visibly wounded.

A fair guess, from the Mandan point of view, of what this party intended, was that they meant to establish a fort or a string of forts somewhere near, or upstream from, the Mandan-Hidatsa villages. Their large boat carried a lot of supplies. The number of men in the party would be sufficient to occupy many fur trading posts, if they were organized in the manner of the Canadians. The Mandan understood the competition between the various companies of white men. This, most likely, represented a strong, competitive move involving the trade in the beavers pelts to which the whites were so unaccountably attracted. The idea that these men were only exploring, taking a look at a path a few miles wide by a few thousand miles long, simply would not have occurred to Sheheke and the other Mandan leaders.

Whatever they thought might be in store, the Mandan decided to approach the strange boat with fighting men holding out a hand of friendship. The warriors picked the spot, a day or more from Mitutanka at the speed the Americans were making. It was a much easier ride from the village. The keelboat flotilla arrived at the island about noon.[60]

The meeting was entirely peaceful and friendly. An unidentified[61] Mandan chief and his brother were among the warriors. After smoking the pipe with the Americans, they took Captain Lewis, the Arikara chief and an interpreter to their tepees. Before the day was through, the chief and his brother rode on the keelboat briefly.

The men from the United States had three boats, two a little familiar to the Mandan, but one unlike anything they had seen before. It was a big boat, fifty-five feet long. It had eleven oars on each side and a deck raised above the hull, making a protected berth beneath. It was a floating fort. The men had an area on deck to which they could retire and return fire if under attack. They had a small cannon mounted on a swivel in the front of the boat and two large guns on swivels in the rear. The boat had a tall wooden spire rising well up above its deck. Ropes were tied to the spire leading both to the boat and hung loosely to the deck. One or more of

"If We Eat, You Shall Eat"

those would come into use when the channel the boat was following narrowed too much for effective use of the oars. Then the ropes
went to shore and were used to pull the boat upriver. There were
forty-six men with Lewis and Clark. One of them was black. Half
the men looked like traders and their engagees, but twenty of them,
scattered throughout the three craft, were military, all similarly
dressed, well-armed, and disciplined. All of the Americans were
disciplined.

After exchanging friendly greetings, the Mandan warriors
smoked with Captain Lewis in "great Cordiallity & Sermony" and
then took Lewis to their camp a mile away. Clark proceeded on,
pushing another four miles upriver before camping below an old
Mandan village. In camp they were visited by more Mandan, who
invited the Arikara chief to join them for the night. He went to
their camp.

More visitors came to see the Americans the following day,
including the son of the late chief of the Mandan. He was missing
fingers and wearing scars as an expression of his grief in losing his
father. They met Coal and Big Man the next day, October 26, just
a short distance from Mitutanka. The two lesser chiefs got a ride on
the keelboat. The Americans turned a bend in the Missouri, heading
west for the first extended stretch in weeks, and then they could see
Mitutanka. It sat high on a plain about fifty feet up from the
Missouri. Palisades ringed it. Harvested fields lay below it. With
crowds coming down to the river, Lewis and Clark came to shore
by one of those harvested gardens. They were met by a curious and
friendly throng of children, women, men, and even the "principal
Chiefs,"[62] which would indicate Sheheke and Little Crow, especially
since Coal and Big Man had been dropped off at their camps some
hours before. Lewis went up to the village with the chiefs and interpreters. Clark, suffering from rheumatism, felt one of them should
stay with the boats until the disposition of the Mandan might reveal
itself. He volunteered to stay put. Lewis was shown to Sheheke's
lodge[63] where they smoked and talked. Then Lewis took them back
to the boat where the chiefs smoked with Clark and poked around
at some of the oddities that came from the United States.

Clark stopped by an unidentified chief's lodge in Mitutanka the next morning, on his way pushing upriver to camp opposite the Knife above Black Cat's village, Nuptadi. He smoked with the chief, but impolitely refused to eat, upsetting his host, who may or may not have been Sheheke. Rene Jessaume smoothed things over as he translated Clark's assurances that the only reason he wasn't eating was that he was indisposed.

The pace of diplomacy was rapid. One day the newcomers were camping in Mitutanka's fields and smoking in its lodges and the next they were visiting other chiefs in other villages. On October 28, Lewis and Clark sped things up even more. They called a general council and invited the leaders of all five villages to attend. Many did, but a high wind came up from the southwest and ruined their plans. No one from Mitutanka could cross the river and the strong winds made the Americans' camp too miserable for a meeting. They put it off for a day and spent a couple hours walking with Black Cat and Jessaume, looking for a well-timbered campsite and discussing the political situation of the five villages.

Big Hidatsa or Menetarra, the home of the Hidatsa Proper with 110 to 130 lodges, served as the anchor for four smaller allied villages built in the years following the 1781 epidemic. Menetarra was by far the largest and was also the northernmost of the villages, built along the west bank of the Knife and bounded on the south by a little creek. The acknowledged leader of the Hidatsa Proper and the principal man in the five villages was Le Borgne, the One Eye, though others held the title of chief in his village. Another group, the Awatixa Hidatsa, were the first Hidatsa people on the Missouri and were also known as the Minnetarees of the Willows. The Awatixa had a long, close relationship with the Mandan. They lived in the village of Metaharta in association with many Mandan families. That mixed-nation village of fifty lodges was also on the west bank of the Knife, just south of Big Hidatsa. Black Moccasin led them. The east river Mandan, mostly of the Nuptadi band, stayed on the east side of the Missouri, building there again. Their village was known as Nuptadi, often written Ruhptaree. It was located below Metaharta and opposite the Wattasoon people's village of Mahawha.

There were forty lodges in Nuptadi Village, Black Cat's village. The Wattasoon were known to themselves as Ahnahways. White traders sometimes called them the Shoe or Moccasin Indians. They had also long been Mandan neighbors and friends. Their village held fifty lodges. All those villages were on the long stretch of river where the Missouri flows mostly due south. A few miles below the parallel villages of Nuptadi and Mahawha the river turns sharply to the east. There, on the south bank of the river, was Sheheke's village. Mitutanka held fifty lodges.[64]

On October 29, the first general council was held and chiefs were acknowledged by Lewis and Clark, though Sheheke was still not present. Neither was Le Borgne, the Hidatsa Proper leader who was the strong man of the five-village metropolitan area. Small presents were handed out to the chiefs in attendance. Lewis gave his speech, one he himself characterized as long. It must have been so. Half of it was too much for Caltarcota, an elder chief of the Hidatsa Proper. Caltarcota showed through his body language that he was eager to be gone from the council before Lewis was halfway through his talk. Lewis was expressing his standard speech to the Indians, one in which he informed his listeners of their place in the new continental order. The United States had obtained sovereignty over your lands, he told tribe after tribe. Your new great father will henceforth supply you with manufactured items, Lewis said. When it looked like Caltarcota was about to bolt, he was chastised by another chief in the council. The old Hidatsa claimed that his discomfort was due to an impending attack on his village by unnamed assailants. His real reason, other than probably feeling too old to put up with long speeches to no practical purpose, was that he could see the end of the talk. The Americans were claiming control over the Knife River village trade, just as Evans had done seven years earlier. The Hidatsa had retained their ties to the Canadian traders then, and they would do so again.

Sheheke, as first chief of his village, was entitled to a Jefferson Peace Medal. He was reportedly out hunting on the 29th and unable to attend the meeting. He got his medal the next day. It carried the visage and name of Thomas Jefferson on one side, on which was stamped the date 1801, and on the other side hands clasped under a sign of an Indian pipe crossed over a tomahawk. The words "PEACE AND FRIENDSHIP" fit into the designs. Sheheke then also got to hear some of the speech Lewis gave on the 29th to the impromptu metro-village council.

Sheheke continued to pursue a good relationship with the Americans in the days that followed. He came to their camp on November 1 to talk about the siting of Fort Mandan, and also offered two generous comments. First, he proclaimed that the Mandan would make peace with the Arikara, as it seemed important to the United States, though Mandan opinion held that the Arikara were both weak and faithless. The Arikara always started the wars, he said, and the Rees (the Arikara) had recently killed a Mandan chief and a pipe carrier sent on a peace mission. When the Mandan were riled, the Arikara were no match for the righteous wrath of the Mandan, he declared. "We kill them like the birds," Sheheke said, "we do not wish to kill more, we will make a good peace."

Sheheke expressed satisfaction that the American's wintering post would be close to his village. "We were sorry when we heard of your going up but now you are going down, we are glad." The proximity would make winter visits for trade and conversation more convenient. It would also put a strong fort nearby, perhaps discouraging raids from other Indians for the winter. Forty-six armed allies made good neighbors in the dangerous world of the Upper Missouri in 1804.

Then White Coyote made his solemn pledge to Lewis and Clark, "If we eat, you shall eat, if we starve, you must starve also." The tradition of Mandan hospitality would not be forgotten. It was more than a generous phrase. Sheheke may have been one of the first to understand the Americans. They were not traditional trading partners. While they were interested in talking about the fur trade, these particular men were not engaged in it. They did not want to trade metal for beaver. That was a very unusual thing for white men. The Knife River villagers found the white obsession with beaver pelts remarkable. Why white men were willing to give away fine scarlet cloth for raw beaver pelts, was something Le Borgne, among others, found difficult to understand. Charles Mackenzie was with Le Borgne and a group of his friends when they began speculating on just how finely clothed the Great Father of the Canadians must be, since he was so free with his cloth. But whether it was understandable, or not, one thing was clear about other white men, they wanted to trap or trade for beaver. This American party was something completely new. They didn't need beaver. But, they were human, so they needed food. Food, the Mandan Nation's first export, was going to be in demand in the winter of 1804–05.

Ironically, if the Americans had accepted the invitation to stay in the lodges of Mitutanka the village would have been responsible for hospitality. The Americans would eat as guests. But, with them slightly removed to their own fort, bartering food for manufactured goods was entirely appropriate. And trade was brisk, though not all exchanges were exercises in barter. Sometimes Mandan hospitality overcame Mandan commercial interests.

Almost two weeks passed before Sheheke visited the American camp again. This time the visit was to their home for the winter. Fort Mandan was under construction. Sheheke and Yellow Corn came to visit on November 12, bringing a generous gift. Yellow Corn was carrying one hundred pounds of fine meat on her back, by Clark's estimate. Conversation, with Jessaume interpreting, turned to the origin of the Mandan, the smallpox epidemic, and the political situation between the Mandan and the other nations of the Upper Missouri. Presumably Sheheke was the source of the information, speaking to Clark through Jessaume. He told of how the Mandan were formerly more numerous in several villages lower down the river, and how the Sioux and other Indians waged war on the Mandan after the earthlodge people were weakened by smallpox. His estimate of warrior strength was that the Mandan could raise about 350 men, the Wattasoons only 80, and the Hidatsa Proper, 600 warriors or more. The Crow had 400 lodges and 1,200 men. He explained some things about language as well, pointing out that the Sioux and Mandan share the same word for water and that the Crow and Hidatsa languages are very similar. Clark heard about the various wars: Crow versus Snake, Hidatsa and Wattasoons versus

Snakes and Sioux. The Mandans, Sheheke related, were "at war with all who make war on them, at present with the Sioux only, and wish to be at peace with all nations."[65]

The rest of November Sheheke stayed away from Fort Mandan. On December 2, a delegation of Mandan chiefs and many young men from Mitutanka brought four Cheyenne representatives to the fort. Sheheke was certainly among them. William Clark said that the Mandan explained and recommended to the Cheyenne, the American Policy, as James Ronda has dubbed it, that the Indian nations should be at peace with one another and friends, trading partners, and allies with the United States. Clark had presents distributed all around, and at about three o'clock the guests left.

Sheheke was back again just five days later, December 7, with hot-breaking and important news. The buffalo herds had started to move from the prairie into the bottoms of the Missouri Valley. The Americans were invited out to join in the hunt with White Coyote and his party. Lewis and fifteen men went out with the Mandan hunters. Patrick Gass, one of Lewis and Clark's sergeants, commented on the nimble footwork of the Indian's horses amongst the angry bison. They would drive the bison to a flat plain, where their horses could work with greatest effect to encircle the herd. Mandan hunters killed thirty or forty buffalo. Lewis and the men killed another eleven animals, but were only able to pack five back to Fort Mandan that day. They observed the Mandan method of determining which hunter was entitled to each animal. Personalized marks on the arrows did the trick.

This little excursion was a very important moment in history. Hunting together is a bonding experience. Enemies don't hunt together. Sheheke reached out a real hand of friendship, not just a rhetorical one, when he took Captain Lewis out hunting. Their relationship was cemented and relations between the United States and the Mandan Nation warmed. From a strictly material view, the act was just as important. It meant that the men of the Corps would eat well. It didn't stop with the five bison brought back to the fort on December 7. Captain Clark got to lead a fifteen-man hunting party the next day, in the bitter cold. They shot another eight bison,

"If We Eat, You Shall Eat"

bringing two home. They left guards winter camping to keep the wolves from stealing their game. Lewis took eighteen men out on December 9, collecting the cached meat and killing ten more buffalo and one deer.

Hunting success slowed considerably in the days that followed. There were some hunting days on which the Americans were shut out and others when only a deer or three might be taken. But Sheheke's invitation had prodded the Americans into action and filled their protein needs for weeks with the small herd they were able to harvest in those first three days. The exposure to Mandan hunting techniques couldn't have hurt, either, as the Corps continued to search for game throughout the winter.

Sheheke had promised, "If we eat, you shall eat." He proved very good to his word.

Visits continued back and forth between the fort and villages. Black Cat was a frequent overnight guest at Fort Mandan. Sheheke and Big Man went to Fort Mandan on December 15. They waited there for Clark to return from an unsuccessful hunt. There were many chiefs and other men, women, and children visiting on December 23 and 24. The quickening pace of guest arrivals, and sleepovers, was broken abruptly on Christmas. The Mandan understood that the Americans wished to observe their Christmas rituals without an audience. They respected the wish so well, they stayed away on the 26th, too.

As the New Year, 1805, approached, the weather turned extremely cold. It was nine below zero on December 29, falling to twenty below on the 30th. Twenty below didn't discourage the Mandan from coming to visit. They were, Clark noted, "much Supprised at the Bellows." The blacksmiths, Privates Shields and Willard, were kept busy turning out useful tools for the Indians that winter, the one added value line of products the Corps could manufacture at Fort Mandan.

On January 1, Sheheke's village rolled out the red carpet for their neighbors. Sixteen men, including Sergeant Ordway, went to Mitutanka to play music and dance at the invitation of the Mandan. Clark went looking for them later to see if everything was going diplomatically. He found an entertaining scene. The Mandan were much pleased by the dancing and music of the white men. Clark asked York to add his feet to the mix, which he did to the delight of the villagers. That such a big man could be so nimble astonished them.

In the midst of the entertainment, a delegation of Mandan leaders returned from aiding with peace negotiations between the Wattasoons and the Hidatsa Proper. Clark was privy to discussion of the immediate cause and peaceful settlement of a dispute that had 150 Hidatsa warriors on their way to exact some punishment on the Wattasoons for the kidnapping, or elopement, of a Hidatsa girl by a Wattasoon young man. The Mandan peacekeepers helped calm the situation. Here was a case where the Mandan could have chosen to be uninvolved, but instead chose to act as peacemakers. Sheheke's peaceful diplomacy reached beyond his own village, his influence helping to protect the weaker Wattasoons from Le Borgne's warriors.

After the conference, and after the dancing, six of the Corps found homes for the evening in Sheheke's village.

On a frigid January 7, Sheheke was a dinner guest at the fort. He stopped by the fort after hunting and was invited to stay and eat. That was the night Clark worked with White Coyote to draw a map. Together they sketched the country between the Knife River villages and the Rockies. Sheheke described the course of the Yellowstone River and placed seven smaller tributaries entering it from the south. The tributary streams included the Big Horn River, Tongue River, Rosebud Creek, Powder River, O'Fallen Creek, and Cabin Creek. The seventh must have been Charbonneau Creek, a tiny trench coming out of what is now the Little Missouri National Grassland in McKenzie County, North Dakota. There's something unexplained about the map, though. On the first draft, reading from east to west, are shown six unnamed streams entering the Yellowstone from the south before coming to the Big Horn River, which is labeled. The map even shows the Little Big Horn's confluence with the Big Horn and a considerable length of the Little Big Horn extending south. That is an accurate count, overlaid on a

"If We Eat, You Shall Eat"

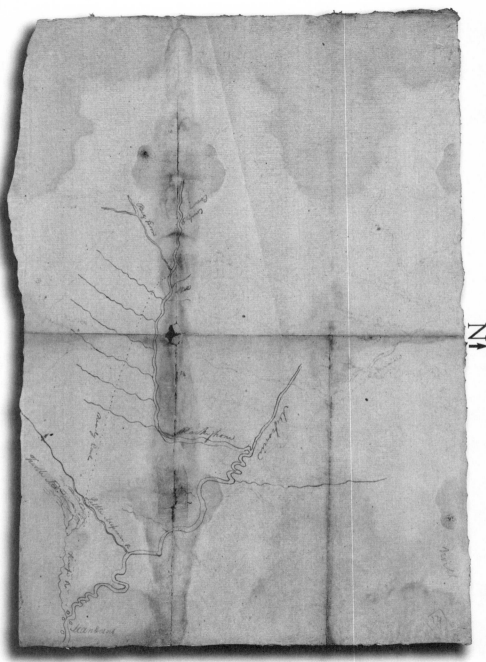

The map Clark and Sheheke produced January 7, 1805 at Fort Mandan, showing the Yellowstone from its confluence with the Missouri to "The High Mountains."

COURTESY OF THE YALE COLLECTION OF WESTERN AMERICANA, BEINECKE RARE BOOK AND MANUSCRIPT LIBRARY

modern map, of the number of creeks and rivers entering the Yellowstone between its mouth on the Missouri and the Big Horn. But on the second draft, a more detailed map, one presumably completed after Clark had traveled down the Yellowstone in 1806, the names of those streams are filled in oddly. Clark places the Tongue River fourth from the east, putting two other streams between it and the Big Horn. Only the Rosebud actually comes between the Tongue and the Big Horn on a modern map. One explanation might be that Clark's Big Horn was what today is called Pryor Creek, near today's Billings, Montana. That would also explain why he shows the Big Horn River running into the Yellowstone on the west side of a range of hills. The Big Horn actually slides by the eastern edge of the Pine Ridge, and Pryor Creek is on the west. Sheheke took the map "as far as the high mountains," says Clark's journal, but unless Clark's designation of the Big Horn was actually Pryor Creek, the extent of the map would only take a traveler to a point where the high mountains could be seen, not experienced. Sheheke told Clark that the country becomes very hilly and heavily timbered. He no doubt piqued Clark's interest when he said the region was filled with beaver and other fur-bearers.

The map work was part of a continuing project of Clark's. He was the expedition's cartographer. Three weeks earlier Clark had received a map, either actual or oral, from Hugh Heney, a fur trader in whom the Captains placed some faith. Heney's contribution described the country to the west of the villages. Sheheke expanded on it and filled in detail. It's unknown whether Sheheke drew a map with his hands or with his voice. From Heney, Clark had obtained "Some Sketches . . . which he had obtained from the Indians to the *West* of this place."[66] If those were on paper, then Sheheke may have been asked to review the existing map and comment on it. Perhaps he traced his own map for Clark, as he explained the nature of the country the Americans would ascend in the spring. Or perhaps the two just talked, along with the resident interpreter Jessaume, and Clark drew as Sheheke remembered lands he had traveled.

In the summer of 1806, Clark would get to race down the Yellowstone Valley. He certainly thought back, as his force paddled

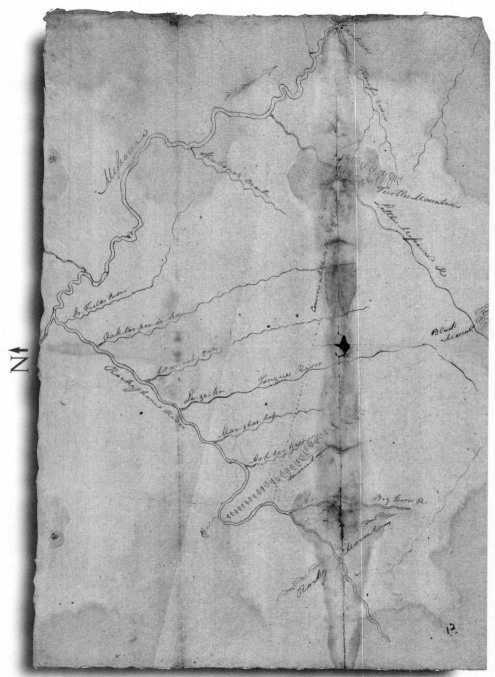

The second "Big White Map," presumably drawn by Clark after his race down the Yellowstone in 1806.

with the current, speeding through the high plains, to the cold night in North Dakota when his Mandan friend had described that country to him.

After the map night, Sheheke doesn't appear in the journals for a month. That may not be at all conclusive that he wasn't in contact with Lewis, Clark, or their men. Only one of the captains wrote each day, almost always William Clark. Many times Indian visitors to Fort Mandan were identified in just that way, as Indian visitors, or as one number or another of Mandan. On at least one specific occasion, it is more likely than not that Sheheke was there. On January 15, four Hidatsa men of considerable note overcame a Mandan ruse and came to Fort Mandan. Some Mandan were already there, as was true most days. A rumor had spread, no doubt from Mandan sources, that the Americans had formed an alliance with the Lakota and were preparing to make war on the Hidatsa. The rumor centered on a few observable facts given a slight twist. Fort Mandan itself was clearly a defensive structure, they pointed out. The Captains had moved the interpreters and their families into the fort. That could be to protect them should war break out. The point of the rumor was to keep the Hidatsa away from the Americans, guaranteeing the Mandan a short-term trading monopoly. It worked for a while, as no Hidatsa came to visit Fort Mandan for more than the first two months of its existence. They had been told, they said the following day when they accused the Mandan of being liars, that the Americans would kill them if they came to the fort. But then, in the middle of January, these four leading men of the Hidatsa had come to see for themselves. Boldly, in front of Lewis and Clark, the four insulted thirty Mandan who visited on the 16th, telling them "they were liars, had told them if they came to the fort the whites men would kill them, they had been with them all night, Smoked in the pipe and have been treated well and the whites had danced for them, observing the Mandans were bad, and ought to hide themselves."[67]

Among the thirty Mandan were six chiefs, by Clark's reckoning. No matter how thinly he sliced the word chief, if there were six of them, all Mandan, Sheheke is more likely than not to have been in the group. The Mandan response was restrained. The four Hidatsa had thrown down the gauntlet, but the Mandan, apparently, let it lay. Clark doesn't sound any note of protest from the Mandan chiefs or others. Their plan had worked. They were satisfied to accept some vaguely directed insults—they don't seem to have been personal—and go on about their business. Peace prevailed.

On February 6, Sheheke and several other prominent men visited Lewis at Fort Mandan. They smoked with him and then left. Lewis found their relatively quick exit uncharacteristic, "for they usually pester us with their good company the balance of the day after once being introduced to our apartment." Perhaps they didn't find his company as welcoming as they found the red-haired chief. Clark had left the fort two days earlier to go on an extended hunting trip. It's not an original perception that Lewis did not appreciate Indian ways as much as his co-captain. The feelings were likely reciprocated. The following day, coincidentally and in the continued absence of William Clark, Captain Lewis issued new orders for Indian guests. None could stay the night at Fort Mandan, other than "those attached to the garrison," which must have meant Sakakawea, Charbonneau's other Shoshone wife, and perhaps Jessaume's wife. The latter had left the fort on January 19 to go to her village and may not have returned by the first week in February. Lewis had a lock put on the gate for the first time, more than two months after the fort's construction.

A party sent out by the Americans on Valentine's Day met with a rough reception. Clark wrote that he sent four men out with horse-drawn sleighs to recover some meat he'd left cached twenty-two miles south of Fort Mandan. The group was assaulted by about 105 Sioux, who treated them rudely and stole two horses and some knives. The American party returned to Fort Mandan that same evening and made their report.

Captain Lewis was determined to show resolve. He decided to set out early the following day in pursuit of the Sioux. Two men were immediately dispatched to inform the Mandans of the incident and request their help, "if any of them chose to pursue those robers." They were told that Lewis would leave early, which he did, setting off at sunrise with twenty-four men from Fort Mandan. The first Mandan to come to help was Sheheke. He arrived about noon. Shortly after, another chief and several other men made it.

Once again, as had been true in December, the Americans were more eager for winter campaigning and punishment of perceived transgressions than were their neighbors. Sheheke showed up, and a handful of others were willing to join with Lewis, but they were in no rush to do it. The white men said they would leave very early on February 16, which turned out to be a fine morning, with the temperature a bracing sixteen degrees below zero. The Indians didn't begin arriving until noon.

Sheheke and the others did join in the pursuit. They caught up to Lewis and participated in his fruitless search. The Sioux had too much of a lead to be caught. Curiously, the joint American-Mandan expedition came upon several pair of moccasins, identified by the Mandan as being of Sioux design. What Lewis' little band would have done, had they found more than a hundred Sioux on the prairie, is unclear. As they walked through the snows on the futile mission, fighting snow blindness, perhaps it occurred to Lewis, as it was certainly clear to Sheheke, that not finding the Sioux might be the best result of the effort. The search was broken off, and the Mandans returned to their villages. Lewis stayed out hunting a couple days more.

Sheheke returned to Fort Mandan on February 21. He and Big Man came for a visit. They told Clark that many of the men of their nation were on a quest to consult the Medicine Stone. Sheheke and Big Man explained the story of the stone. The Medicine Stone, a rocky outcropping on the prairie about eighty miles, or three days travel, southwest of the Knife River villages, is a sacred place to the Mandan, and to other Indian peoples as well.[68] It served as an oracle. The Mandan would ride to the stone and reverently offer it smoke. They would then retire to camp nearby, returning the following day. There they would find raised white marks on the rock which would be interpreted to give the visitors a glimpse into the near future, or as Clark says, "to know What was to be the result of the insuing year. They have great confidence in this Stone and Say that it informs them of every thing which is to happen, & visit it every Spring & Sometimes in the Summer." The two chiefs gave Clark a thorough description of the stone and its importance in Mandan planning for the coming year.

The pace of preparations for the next leg of the Lewis and Clark expedition picked up as hints of spring came to the Knife River region. Clark's journal entries became briefer and focused on activities like freeing the pirogues from the ice. Hidatsa visits became more frequent too, pushing the solid relations the Captains had built with Sheheke and his village into the background, at least as far as the journal entries go. It may be, it's likely in fact, that by late February, Lewis and Clark felt assured of the friendship of Sheheke and began to take that relationship for granted as they tried to extend their diplomacy into more troublesome quarters.

The Arikara sent word that arrived at Fort Mandan on February 28, that they were fed up with being neighbors to the Lakota and were considering a move north to join the Mandan in a common defense against the nomadic bands. They wondered if they would be welcomed. This was music to the ears of Lewis and Clark, who passed the word along to the Mandan at Mitutanka, Sheheke's village. The Mandan response came quickly and represented the same position they had consistently held since the Americans had first started talking to them about inter-tribal peace. Sheheke's promise to make a good peace was still the national policy. The Mitutanka leaders who responded to the Arikara query said that they had always wished for peace and to be good neighbors to the Arikara. The other nations at the Knife River villages would have the same opinion, the Mandan believed. Sheheke, certainly, was influential in helping to shape the Mandan response to the Arikara proposal. He was most likely the proposal's spokesman.

Black Cat heard about the Arikara initiative on March 3, at Fort Mandan, as flocks of ducks and geese were heading north in their seasonal migration. He returned again the next day, this time with Sheheke, who brought the Americans a present of meat. It was a small present, according to Clark, but one probably much appreciated because of its timing. The pickings from hunting had been slim in late winter. In the cycle of seasons on the Northern Plains, the hungriest time is always early spring. Garden food stores have been declining for six months by the time March rolls around. Game, when it can be found, is skinny after a winter of meager subsistence. Sheheke's gift could not have been more timely.

The next mention of Sheheke in the journals, and the last one in 1805, comes on March 19. He came to the fort with Little Crow and a Mandan couple who had a sick child. Clark administered some care for the young one and counciled with the two chiefs. The Hidatsa, he was informed, had already sent out two war parties and a third was planning to head out. These parties would be heading the same direction as the Corps of Discovery intended to travel. Clark couldn't have been pleased to hear that they could soon be traveling through a war zone.

During the following eighteen days, the Americans were in a rush to prepare for their trip to the Pacific. There was still much visiting back and forth, but journal entries shrank in an inverse relationship to the duties of the Captains. Very few individual Indians are mentioned by name over that period. On April 6, not quite five and a half months after they had arrived, Lewis and Clark left the Mandan and headed upriver. They took from the villages only Charbonneau, Sakakawea and their baby, Jean Baptiste. One unidentified Mandan man trailed along for a day, and then returned to his village.

Charbonneau was chosen over Jessaume for a simple reason: his wife. Jessaume's wife was Mandan and his own language skills were shaped by that relationship. Charbonneau didn't speak any language particularly well according to some accounts, but he could communicate in Hidatsa with Sakakawea, and in French with several of the Corps. He spoke some English, too. Sakakawea spoke Hidatsa and, importantly, Shoshone. As the Corps reached Shoshone country, that would prove critical.

There is no record of a farewell scene when the Americans said goodbye to Sheheke in 1805. At that moment, neither party was certain they would see the other again. Sheheke knew some of the dangers lying in front of Lewis and Clark, and he could imagine more. The Captains were uncertain about their mode of return to the United States. They had some hopes of meeting an ocean-going ship on the Pacific Coast, and then returning by way of the Straits of Magellan. If that did not transpire, they thought they might return to the Upper Missouri by winter.

Sheheke had invested much in the Americans, though nothing he could not afford to be without. He had held out a hand of friendship, and that hand was shaken in friendship. His diplomatic goals were clear and simple. At first, he wanted the Corps to locate either within his village or nearby, for mutual defense and ease of trade. That goal was accomplished when Fort Mandan was sited across the river from Mitutanka. His second goal was to encourage a short-term profitable commerce with the Americans. This was also quickly accomplished, as his people traded relatively abundant and ultimately renewable food stores for the unique and durable goods of the United States. Thirdly, he wished to make long-term friendships with the Americans. Through the winter, generally at two week intervals, he visited them. He invited them to hunt in the Mandan style. He brought them food. And, he brought the Captains information, a lot of information. He instructed them in the political currents of the Northern Plains. He helped Clark draw a map of the region the Americans were intending to explore. Sheheke told them stories about history, religion, and social mores. He was, their own preference for Black Cat's "perspicacity" notwithstanding, the single best friend the Americans made at the Mandan and Hidatsa villages. When Clark wanted to mount a military expedition, he went to Sheheke's lodge to talk it over. When Lewis did set off on a foolish military mission, Sheheke was the first Indian to join in. Sheheke was not the most feared warrior of the five villages. He was not particularly eager for battle, and he certainly knew that Lewis was being an idiot to march blindly, literally as snow blindness affected the pursuit, across the snow with a force of twenty-four men in search of a party of Sioux more than four times that size. But Sheheke joined in. He demonstrated to Lewis and Clark that he was willing to fight at their side. The alliance between the United States and the Mandan was made, at that moment, real. It was not just words.

Sheheke, the civil chief, put his life on the line, a volunteer enlistee in an American campaign.

As he watched them paddle upriver, Sheheke the diplomat must have wondered if any of his efforts had been worthwhile. The Americans' visit might have been like Evans', just a fleeting mirage. As a diplomat, the results of his actions were uncertain in April of 1805.

7

The Mandan Ambassador

The Americans had been long gone when 1806 dawned. The Mandan were probably not too surprised that Lewis and Clark hadn't come back to winter with them again, though that was President Jefferson's presumption. Jefferson expected that they had gone to the Pacific Coast and returned to winter somewhere on the Upper Missouri within six or eight months.[69] It would be natural for them to return to their proven safe haven. But the Mandan might have known better. Even if no Mandan had ever traveled to the Pacific, and that is by no means certain, the Mandan knew that a horseback round-trip to the Rockies took months, and they knew there were numerous nations west in the high country. Through many conversations during the winter of 1804–05, Lewis and Clark had discussed their plans with their hosts. The Mandan were well aware of the plans to go to the Pacific. They were also aware that the Americans anticipated a probable return visit that winter. With a more realistic view of the distances and difficulties, the immense and tedious effort the Rockies required, the Mandan may not have been surprised that the Americans didn't return in the winter. Their absence through the winter of 1805 did not mean they were lost or not coming back. Still, the American presence was out of sight, and that meant business went on as usual. The trading relationships forged in the previous century remained operative. There were free traders and men from Hudson's Bay Company in residence in the villages as 1806 opened. There was scarcely a time that year, or for any significant length of time in any year from at least 1794 on, that there was not at least one Canadian trading party resident at the villages.[70]

In the summer of 1806, Alexander Henry the Younger made his way from the Red River to the Missouri. Henry was a manager of the North West Company's interests in the Red River region, but his mission, as he explained to the Mandan and Hidatsa, was not of trade, but merely of curiosity. After Lewis and Clark's visit, his claim had some credibility to the villagers. The curiosity was that given Henry's tendency toward the ethnocentric, he should be curious enough about a Native American culture to voluntarily fight muck, mire, and mosquitoes to see their homes doesn't seem in character. But clearly it was, because there he was, struggling across the hot, wet prairie in July on his way to see for himself the legendary Mandan.

Dozens, maybe hundreds, of white men had visited the Knife River metropolitan area in the sixty-eight years prior to Henry's arrival, but none described the community scene quite as he did. Henry thought the people and their customs less than commendable, but found their nation as a whole very pastoral and surprisingly "civilized."

> . . . we proceeded on a delightful hard, dry road. The soil being a mixture of sand and clay, and rain being infrequent, the heat of the sun makes the road as hard as pavement. Upon each side were pleasant cultivated spots, some of which stretched up the rising ground on our left, whilst on our right they ran nearly to the Missouri. In those fields were many women and children at work, who all appeared industrious. Upon the road were passing and repassing every moment natives, afoot and on horseback curious to examine and stare at us. Many horses

were feeding in every direction beyond the planta-
tion. The whole view was agreeable, and had more
the appearance of a country inhabited by a civilized
nation than by a set of savages.[71]

Henry met Sheheke, of course. A prestigious visitor to the five
villages made the rounds. He also met Black Cat, Big Man, Hairy
Horn, Le Borgne, and many others chiefs. Coming from the northeast, the first village Henry visited was the only one on the east
bank of the Missouri, Black Cat's Nuptadi Village. Henry spent the
night in the Tixopinic, which he assumed to be a guest house of
Black Cat's, cared for by one of the chief's wives. He paid careful
attention to the nude bathing habits of the villagers, being shocked
by the female immodesty that evening and checking again in the
morning just to see if he'd gotten it right. His journal entry for the
day of July 19, 1806, is filled with details of Mandan nudity and sex-
ual behavior. After noting how unconcerned Mandan women were
with walking naked in front of men of all ages, including passing
quite close to his own viewing spot, Henry recorded how he was
forced to disappoint, or perhaps insult, several young women who
wished to sleep with him. Then, at midnight, he peeked out of his
lodge to see the cause of some riotous commotion. There were two
dozen young men and women carousing playfully on the village
plaza. Henry watched for a time and paid close enough attention to
their behavior to note that they paired off in intimate relations occasionally before rejoining the larger group. It was a social behavior
unobserved by Henry in the other Indian nations he knew. He
believed the semi-public couplings by young people on a summer
evening were driven by the elders of the lodges locking their doors
to intruding young men. Not being able to sneak in, the suitors sat
out on the lodges and played music to beckon their favorite girls to
come out and play.

Henry's view of Mandan bathing habits is somewhat at odds
with George Catlin's description written nearly three decades later.
Maybe it was time passing and social mores changing. Maybe it was
a difference between the Nuptadi villagers and the Mitutankans.

Certainly, Henry was more uptight and ethnocentric than Catlin. At Mitutanka, in 1832, Catlin saw two different bathing areas, one for women and girls and another for men and boys.

> At the distance of half a mile or so above the village, is the customary place where the women and girls resort every morning in the summer months, to bathe in the river. To this spot they repair by hundreds, every morning at sunrise, where, on a beautiful beach, they can be seen running and glistening in the sun, whilst they are playing their innocent gambols and leaping into the stream.[72]

Men armed with bows and arrows kept sentinel over the women, said Catlin, "to guard and protect this sacred ground from the approach of boys or men from any directions." The men had their own bathing spot, a little distance below the village.

After Henry's fitful evening, the next morning, July 20, Jean Baptiste LaFrance came over to Nuptadi Village from Mitutanka. LaFrance, a Canadian free trader, had been residing in Sheheke's village for a couple of months. He helped Henry converse more fully with Black Cat. Getting the word that Henry was an important man in the Canadian fur business and was truly just there to visit—to learn more about the Mandan—Black Cat had a funny response. He went back to his lodge and brought out the American flag given to him by Lewis and Clark twenty months before. Black Cat had the flag flown outside Henry's guest lodge. He then showed Henry some other gifts from the Americans. He showed the Canadian that he was friends with the Americans. There are two possible reasons why he did that. Perhaps Black Cat was demonstrating simply that he got along well with white people, was recognized as an important friend of white people and that Henry could therefore count on him to be a useful friend and ally. Or, he may have been telling Henry the score. Black Cat is a friend of the Americans. Canadians are welcome here, they will be well treated here, but we are friends with the Americans. Given the fact that Lewis and Clark had been gone for fifteen months, the former seems like a more reasonable motivation for an intelligent leader like Black Cat. The former is polite and welcoming, the latter needlessly confrontational. The former is the more typical Mandan response though it also shows Black Cat as less than perspicacious in his understanding of Canadian-American tensions.

Assailed by people eager to trade, Henry dismissed as futile the idea of asking Black Cat to arrange bullboats to transfer his party south to the other side of the river. He recognized to some extent the complex political landscape of the five independent villages. Thinking the Nuptadians would seek to monopolize his time, even if they believed he had no goods, he asked LaFrance to arrange transport across the river from the people of Mitutanka. Eight bull-boats came across, with eight men to assist in getting Henry's group over. One of those men was Sheheke, introduced to the Canadians as the chief of Mitutanka, piloting his own boat.

Sheheke took Henry and Charles Chaboillez, Jr., in his craft. Chaboillez was another North West Company trader. As they spun in the Missouri currents, Henry could see that there were two American flags in view. One still topped Black Cat's lodge, where Henry had spent the previous night. The other was in Mitutanka. Sheheke explained that the flag was flying over his own lodge and had been given to him by Lewis and Clark.

Big Man met the boats on shore and escorted the Canadians to his lodge. When it came time to break up the party for the night, so as not to overburden any single host, the white men were sent to the lodges of several prominent men. Sheheke was not among them. Henry was questioned about that the following day by Sheheke. He was, Henry believed, insulted that none of the Canadians took advantage of his hospitality.

It's a wonder they hadn't. Sheheke was clearly a leading man of the Mandan. The American flag would have indicated to Henry that Lewis and Clark, at least, considered him the top chief of Mitutanka. Maybe it can be inferred from the slight that there was a perception among the Canadian traders that there was a pro-American faction at Mitutanka, and that Sheheke was its leader. But Henry showed no similar insult to Black Cat, who was an American favorite. And Henry was quick to make amends to Sheheke by making him gifts of tobacco and ammunition. Most likely it was the American flag that kept the Englishmen out of the chief's lodge, although it may have just been miscommunication, an oversight, or the work of a competing faction in the village.

Henry, like Clark eighteen months earlier, was witness to a Mandan council at Mitutanka, some preliminary peace talks with an Arikara delegation. Six young representatives of the Arikara rode into Mitutanka not long after Henry arrived. Their appearance caused quite a stir and led Henry to believe that the Arikara party might be killed by enraged villagers. Henry got a lesson in Plains diplomacy.

The Arikara were there to forestall a threatened offensive by the Mandan and Hidatsa. Some Arikara warriors had previously accompanied a body of Sioux in an attack on a Mandan hunting party which resulted in the deaths of five Mandan men. A punitive war party had ridden out from the Mandan villages, accompanied by their Hidatsa allies. They didn't find the Sioux, but did kill two Arikara. That was unsatisfactory revenge, however, and word had been sent to the Arikara to expect another visit in the fall.

The other villages were notified of the arrival of the delegation. In the council that ensued, probably in the Tixopinic, discussion was brief. However the Mandan had received the Arikara entreaties, the Hidatsa were not ready to talk. They rode in, a band of thirty warriors flying at top speed and dismounting with a bad attitude. The Hidatsa told the Arikara to go home. If their nation truly wanted peace, the Arikara war chief Red Tail would need to personally appear. They gave the Arikara two months to consider the situation. If peace was not settled with Red Tail, in person and before the end of the harvest, Mandan and Hidatsa warriors would come calling.

A few weeks after Henry's visit, from a camp set convenient to several of the Knife River villages, Lewis and Clark made their presence felt again. During a three day period, August 14–16, in the month of the Ripe Wild Plums, William Clark conducted negotiations to secure a delegation of Mandan and Hidatsa chiefs to travel to Washington City to meet President Jefferson. First to get an invitation was Clark's favorite, Black Cat. While the Corps established their campsite, Clark walked up to Nuptadi Village, which he noticed had changed considerably. The village had been rebuilt, Clark thought, and was now much smaller than it had been less than a year and a half earlier. Some of Black Cat's people had quarreled and, in accord with Mandan tradition, had separated from the village. They had gone over to the other side of the river. It's not clear whether the quarreling families moved into Mitutanka or began the establishment of another village.

Clark broached the subject of Black Cat and some of the other principal chiefs accompanying the Corps of Discovery on its return to the United States. The Mandan chief acknowledged that he would like to visit the United States and meet the Great Father, but he was afraid of the Sioux, "who were yet at war with them, and were on the river below and would certainly kill him if he attempted to go down."[73] Clark assured Black Cat that the Americans could and would protect "any of our red children who should think proper to accompany us." He also promised great riches to the ones brave enough to go, saying that the presents they could expect would be very liberal. Black Cat agreed only to provide some corn to the Americans the following day, Mandan hospitality still in evidence despite the fact that the Americans had run dry of trade goods.

Clark returned to his encampment where he entertained Le Borgne and several other chiefs. A council was held at a flat spot on the riverbank. The pipe was passed and then Clark gave a "harangue," as Nicholas Biddle put it, to the effect that the United States dearly wanted to return the hospitality they had experienced from the Mandan and Hidatsa. Le Borgne responded by noting that the Sioux were in the way and would certainly kill any of them who accepted the invitation. Le Borgne delivered a harangue of his own about the emptiness of any peace with the Sioux. Eight Hidatsa had been killed in fights with the Sioux since Lewis and Clark had gone west. Both the Sioux and Arikara had stolen horses. The Hidatsa had been forced to kill two Arikara in retaliation. If there was a real peace with the southern nations he would be glad to go with them to meet the Great Father, Le Borgne said, but as there was not, it was not going to happen.

This was tough medicine for Clark. The American Policy didn't seem to be taking hold, and there was no question that the Corps was headed home in a hurry. The explored-out party of men who could certainly almost taste the whiskey of St. Louis by this time weren't interested in long periods of diplomacy. The one task that remained took on even more importance, a willing delegate must be found.

Clark tried Black Cat again on August 15. Accepting the invitation to come over and pick up some corn, Clark went to Nuptadi. An even more urgent plea for any Mandan delegate met with disappointment in Black Cat's village. Though Clark had spun a promise that the President would provide *"bountifull gifts,"* Black Cat would not go, and he warned that the path home for the Corps was so "dangerous none of this village would go down." A young man contradicted his chief by stepping forward to offer his services. The leaders of Nuptadi quickly quashed that idea, telling Clark that the young man's character was questionable.

Back at camp, Clark received good news. Little Crow, the war chief of Mitutanka, would go with the expedition. Charbonneau and Clark walked down to the village to talk it over with him. Little Crow said that he was interested, in fact, determined, to go down, but that he wanted to discuss it with a village council that afternoon. They smoked on it.

The following morning, August 16, a council convened at about ten o'clock at Lewis and Clark's encampment. Clark gave a speech mixing a respectful tone with criticism. "I had listened with much attention to what the One Eye had said yesterday and beleived that he was sincere & Spoke from his heart. I reproached them very severely for not attending to what had been said to them by us in council . . ." Clark pointed to incidents of Hidatsa attacks on the "pore defenceless" Shoshone and the Arikara troubles.

Old Calcorata, Little Cherry, who had been so antsy during Lewis' long oration in October 1804, took his turn with Clark.

He portrayed the Hidatsa as the party sinned-against. Ignoring the charge about the Hidatsa Proper raiding the Shoshone, the chief repeated what Le Borgne had said about the Lakota and Arikara attacks on Hidatsa horses and persons. Calcorata softened though and promised to "attend to your word and not hurt any people. All shall be welcome and we shall do as you direct." Le Borgne chimed in, too, with a promise to keep his ears open to the words of the American President. Neither would go to meet him, however, and no other Hidatsa would either. The meeting disbanded with one final ceremony: Le Borgne was presented with the Corps' swivel gun, a gift of U.S. arms to a man Lewis and Clark hoped would be a U.S. ally.

Clark went to Mitutanka to confirm arrangements with Little Crow and to present him with an American flag. Clark was shocked when he found Little Crow had changed his mind. A disagreement with Sheheke had somehow discouraged him from accepting the American offer. He refused to accept the flag. Clark asked to speak with Rene Jesseaume. The Métis trader and translator was dispatched to see if he could talk a chief into joining the group. He only needed to talk to one.

Sheheke knew the dangers of passing the Indians below were real. The men who had turned the offer down were anything but cowards. They were brave chiefs, and realistic. Still, the voyage presented itself as an exciting, daring, and fascinating trip. It would be a high point in Sheheke's career, and, although dangerous, this would be an extremely important diplomatic mission. It was unprecedented, really, in the level of responsibility being entrusted to White Coyote. Most diplomatic conversations were large group meetings with many leaders from each nation present and most involved in the discussions. Being alone, Sheheke would not be able to consult with his friends and other chiefs. Specific negotiations would not be possible.

He could though, and would, become strictly an ambassador of goodwill. He would carry the message to the United States and to other nations met along the way that the Mandan wanted peace and friendship. That position was a fair representation of their national

policy since 1781, if not long before. The Mandan had been seriously weakened by disease and refugee status. The loss of young men in
warfare was becoming a serious matter, threatening the very ability
of the two Mandan villages to remain independent.

White Coyote probably held little hope that the numerous and
aggressive Lakota peoples would agree to a real and lasting peace
with the Mandan. He knew that the Arikara might be well-disposed
to hear the words of peace. They often did listen. But relations with
the Arikara had a predictable pattern. Talks led to peace, peace was
fleeting and gave way to war, which led to talks, which led to peace.
Peace was fleeting.

Although unlikely, it was at least conceivable he would find allies
beyond the lands of the Arikara and Lakota. The Pawnee were close
to the Arikara, and therefore probably hostile to the Mandan, but
the Omaha people were of the same Siouan and earthlodge tradition as the Mandan. They might be inclined to be friendly. But, certainly, the best reason to go was to cement the relationship with
these men of the United States. If their stories were true and they
were coming to the Upper Missouri to challenge the British traders,
and since they had demonstrated that they were strong enough to
force their way through the nations along the river downstream,
they would make excellent allies and trading partners.

By going, White Coyote would advance the cause of all the
Knife River villages. But his own village would benefit the most,
particularly if he went with Lewis and Clark while Black Cat's village and the Hidatsa villages sent no representatives. Personally, two
strong motivations presented themselves. The first was travel, natural
human curiosity about other people and other places. The second
was the opportunity to build status and gain added prominence for
himself and his family. Of course, accepting the invitation could
mean accepting a death sentence for himself and his family, Yellow
Corn and the toddler, White Painted Lodge. In the end, weighing
the risks and benefits, White Coyote made the patriotic decision.

The trip was risky, a gamble, but a chance worth taking for his
people. Life was not in balance at Mitutanka the way it had been in
his youth at On-a-Slant. Not only had smallpox ravaged the popula-

tion two decades prior, and perhaps six years before, but even in that spring of 1806 disease had struck again with dire consequences, particularly for the very young and old. Whooping cough killed 130 villagers in less than a month. More young men were dying in battle these days than were being raised to take their places. One Eye bullied the Mandan, and Sheheke's people had to accept it and eat crow. It had become ever more dangerous to hunt in traditional spots away from the villages. Life had once been better.

Little Crow and Sheheke reconciled their differences and it was agreed that Sheheke would travel to the United States while the war chief maintained village security. Sheheke and Jesseaume agreed that they would be unhappy to be away from their wives and children on such a long and uncertain trek. The two men decided that Sheheke would agree to the invitation only if the Captains would agree to take their families along as well. Lewis and Clark easily agreed.

The following day Lewis and Clark left their camp by the first Hidatsa village and traveled downriver to Mitutanka. The other chiefs had come to see Sheheke off. They clustered at the riverbank, near the Americans' boat. White Coyote and his friends were in his lodge when the Captains arrived. They sat in a circle, smoking. Nearby, Yellow Corn cried with her female companions. When Clark came into the lodge, Sheheke sent his wife and son and their baggage to the boat. Jessaume, his wife, and their children went along with them. White Coyote lingered. He distributed gifts to his friends, sharing with them some of the powder and ball he had received from the Americans.

Then, to bless the endeavor, Sheheke broke out his pipe again. Clark smoked with him and then they headed down to the riverbank, accompanied by the entire village.

Some cried over saying goodbye to their chief. Captain Clark went through the crowd, shaking hands with the head men of each village. They requested he smoke with them one last time, which he did. After the pipe had been passed, one chief rose and told Clark that when his force had first come up the river, the Indians did not believe all that they were told. But seeing them return and having no reason to doubt them, the villages would remember carefully all they had been told and follow the advice of the Americans. The others agreed and assured Clark that he could report to the Great Father that the young men would remain at home and not make war on any people except in defense of themselves.

One Eye patronizingly directed Clark to take good care of his chief, as if Sheheke was his vassal. Clark said that they would take special care of Sheheke and his family and that he would be sure to inform the Arikara of the Mandan and Hidatsa peoples' desire to hold a parlay with them and the other nations of the region to establish a general peace on the Northern Plains.

Finally aboard, the party fired the swivel gun in salute and the expedition let the current take them the short jaunt to the old site of Fort Mandan. It was largely destroyed. A fire had consumed all but one apartment. They camped there for the night, the Americans surely a little melancholy for their old winter home, and set out again a little after eight the next morning.

The boats the expedition used in 1806 were nothing like the large keelboat that had so amazed the villagers two years previous. They were instead floating in hollowed out tree trunks, pirogues of their own manufacture. The Americans had lashed each pair together to make stable river craft.

Shortly after the canoes were launched from Fort Mandan, an Indian was seen running down to the riverbank hallooing to get their attention. Sheheke noticed him and told Jesseaume that it was his brother and he needed to talk with him. They put to shore. White Coyote said his goodbye to his brother, gave him a prized pair of leggings, and the two separated in what was described as a most affectionate manner.

Through Jesseaume, Sheheke acted as travel guide for the first few days of the trip. He kept up a commentary for the crew about the old villages and natural formations they passed. He told them about the history and culture of the Mandan and about significant places in their old homeland. On the evening of August 20, camped across from the ruins of On-a-Slant, Sheheke told them that he had been born in that village forty years prior. He told them about the origin of the Mandan in that village under the earth.

A few days later, the boat pulled to shore at the upper village of the Arikara, about twelve miles above the place where the Grand River enters the Missouri. The Americans and the Mandan chief held a cordial council with the Arikara there, and with a band of Cheyenne who happened to also be present, trading for the harvest bounty. Though the Cheyenne had abandoned the farming way of life they practiced along the James River centuries before, they had never lost their appreciation for corn.

Past the Arikara villages, through plains dominated by the Lakota and the Dakota, the boats swept on. Though he knew the situation to be dangerous, Sheheke was probably reassured by the attitude of the Americans. These were solid men, disciplined adventurers who had traveled in far countries among vastly more numerous strangers. They were alert, but not nervous as they passed early fall hunting parties on both sides of the Missouri.

On a momentous day, September 20, the white men raised a shout of joy. "Cattle," they cried. Several creatures grazing on shore appeared to Sheheke as diminutive and short-haired bison. But his traveling companions were very excited. White Coyote might have wondered if it was because the animals were good to eat and easy to hunt. Jessaume would have explained that the white men were happy because the cattle, domesticated herd animals, were a sign that their nation was near.

The flotilla arrived a little later at the outpost of La Charette, or Charriton. The men of the expedition hollered and whooped as they pulled to shore. The men asked for and received permission to fire their guns in salute. Three rounds were fired and a hearty cheer raised. The enthusiasm of the Corps was tempered somewhat when they found the price on shore was an exorbitant eight dollars cash for two gallons of whiskey.

On they proceeded to St. Charles, arriving about three in the afternoon on the following day. It was Sunday afternoon and the gentlemanly set and their ladies were strolling. Sheheke took it all in, the women's clothes, particularly, different from any he had seen. It began to dawn on the Mandan chief that the culture he was beginning to observe bore little relation to the culture the

Americans had shown him on this voyage or during the Fort Mandan winter.

On September 22, they stopped at Cantonment Bellefontaine. Colonel Thomas Hunt ordered Lieutenant Peters to fire the camp's artillery in salute. The Captains obtained some American-style clothing for White Coyote. Yellow Corn retained her traditional dress. At about ten on the following day, September 23, White Coyote saw St. Louis for the first time. He would return to it at least twice in the following years.

Word had spread that the Corps of Discovery had been sighted and was coming in from Cantonment that morning. As *Western World*, the newspaper of Frankfort, Kentucky, put it, "the great concourse of people that lined the bank of the river at the time of their landing at this place [St. Louis] the next day, must be considered as a strong evidence of the respect entertained of those gentlemen for the danger and difficulties they must have encountered in their expedition of discovery."

In 1806 St. Louis was a town of about 1,000 people. There were two hundred homes, many very large and built of stone. The town was built on high ground, which was considered a healthy choice. The leading people of the town lived very well and though it was still a frontier town, it had a decided French influence. Clothing styles, therefore, were of some importance. Though Sheheke was now an Indian in American clothing, the Americans he traveled with were dressed more like Indians than even people in this frontier town were used to seeing. "They really have the appearance of Robinson Crusoes dressed entirely in buckskin," one commentator thought.

St. Louis was not much bigger in population than Sheheke's village, and only a quarter the size of the five-village metropolis. Though it was a frontier town, its surrounding farms, its streets and variety of buildings, and its very active riverfront were like nothing Sheheke had seen before. Other Mandans had visited cities—the Mandan children who were taken to Montreal by la Verendrye's lieutenant, for instance. But none on record had returned to tell of what they'd seen.

Lewis and Clark and all their men were greeted enthusiastically and given great hospitality by the St. Louians. Many expressed their joy and relief that the expedition had returned safely after some had given them up for dead or hopelessly lost in the mysterious West. At a grand party thrown in their honor, following dinner at Cristy's Inn, on September 25, Lewis and Clark joined in the first seventeen toasts, an account of which survived and was uncovered by historian James Ronda. As Ronda pointed out, "The list of toasts alone is worth the price of admission."[74] The assembled dignitaries bent elbows first to President Jefferson, "the friend of science, the polar star of discovery, the philosopher and the patriot." They went on to drink to the President's cabinet and other bureaucrats, to the "Missouri expedition—may the knowledge of the newly explored regions of the West, be the least benefit that we may derive from this painful and perilous expedition," and to the men who followed Lewis and Clark into the great Northwest. They drank, too, to the Territory of Louisiana and to the United States, with a puzzling comment, "Whilst they tolerate a spirit of enquiry, may never forget, that united they stand, but divided they fall."

As the toasts piled up, the toasters reached farther for appropriate topics. The seventh toast was to the memory of Christopher Columbus, apparently inspired by comparison to Lewis and Clark. A clause of that toast rings hauntingly predictive of Lewis' later troubles, "May those who imitate his hardihood, perseverance and merit, never have, like him, to encounter public ingratitude."

They continued to drink, toasting the Constitution and hoping that its tenets would reach to the ends of the earth. They drank to Washington, the man, and another toast to Washington, the city. "Peace with all nations; but submission to none," came eleventh on the list. Commerce, Agriculture, and Industry covered two more drinks. Revolutionary War veterans were remembered, too. "The Missouri—Under the auspices of America, may it prove a vehicle of wealth to all the nations of the world," and a call for the national government to be always under the influence of true Republicanism instead of private ambition and political intrigue were the fifteenth and sixteenth toasts. The seventeenth, and last before Lewis and

Clark took their leave, was a tip of the hat to the ladies present, "The fair daughters of Louisiana—may they ever bestow their smiles on hardihood and virtuous valor."

Finally, after the Captains had been excused from the gathering, and walked, or been helped, out the door, a final toast was raised to the explorers, "Captains Lewis and Clark—Their perilous services endear them to every American heart."[75]

Indian chiefs visited St. Louis with enough frequency that not much fuss seems to have been made over White Coyote. Sheheke being a Mandan chief, however, may have sparked a renewed interest in the commercial possibilities of trade in the Upper Missouri country. In the years following the successful return of Lewis and Clark, Manuel Lisa, Pierre Chouteau, Pierre Dorian, and many others would attempt to work in the Mandan region, with varying levels of success.

St. Louis was at the frontier of the vast American nation. The distance traveled from Mitutanka to St. Louis, 1,100 miles, was not nearly so great as the distance still remaining for Sheheke to travel, from St. Louis to the American capital, 1,600 miles, where lived their Great Father. The Captains said goodbye to most of their men and then set off for Vincennes, capital of Indiana, where they were warmly greeted by the Governor. The expedition had gotten smaller; Lewis and Clark traveled with Sergeant Matthew Ordway, York, Sheheke, Yellow Corn, the baby, Rene Jessaume's family, Francis Labiche, Pierre Chouteau, and some Osage chiefs.[76]

It was October 1806 by the time they reached Cahokia, a new American town set close by an ancient Indian city. More people lived in the first Cahokia than lived in the entire Mandan Nation at its height, before the smallpox. Abandoned long before the Americans came, Cahokia had been a center for dispersal of corn culture throughout the Midwest and up the Missouri.

Then it was on to Louisville for a big banquet and ball. The new celebrity, William Clark, now measured up to his formerly more famous relative, George Rogers Clark, who eagerly soaked up the tales of the Rockies and beyond. Captain Clark and York left the traveling group there, while Lewis and White Coyote, with Jessaume and their families, Sergeant Ordway, and Francis Labiche went by the Old Wilderness Road on to Frankfort, Kentucky, reaching that town on November 13 and leaving on November 15.[77] Lewis accepted a commission to survey the Walker Line between Virginia and Kentucky while traveling through. The Virginian's survey gained a ten-mile strip of disputed land for his home state.

On December 11, the party reached Staunton, Virginia.[78] Two days later they were at the Lewis home, Locust Hill, for a family reunion.[79] When they finally reached Charlottesville they may have found time to visit Monticello. Jefferson had encouraged Lewis to do that. In a letter dated October 26, and posted to Charlottesville to intercept Lewis, the third president sent a message to be delivered to Sheheke.[80]

"Tell my friend of Mandane also that I have already opened my arms to receive him. Perhaps while in our neighborhood, it may be gratifying to him, & not otherwise to yourself to take a ride to Monticello and see in what manner I have arranged the tokens of friendship I have received from his country particularly as well as from other Indian friends: that I am in fact preparing a kind of Indian hall."

Jefferson suggested the final route to the capital for Lewis to follow. He wished to show off to Sheheke the cities of Richmond, Fredericksburg, and Alexandria, something "none of the others have visited," and to demonstrate the convenience of public stage travel in the young republic. That route took Sheheke along the Potomac, wide as a bay of the Chesapeake south of Washington City. On December 28, after more than four months travel from Mitutanka, the party reached the capital city of the United States. They rested.

8

The Wolf in Washington

On December 30, Sheheke paid a state visit to the Presidential Mansion, not yet known as the White House. No doubt the Mandan chief and his entourage arrived by horse-drawn carriage, a mode of transportation he was surely getting used to, though it was one he hadn't seen, or perhaps even imagined in his first forty years. The streets through which the Mandan party rumbled were muddy. Washington was a muddy little town in 1806, and the President's yard was no exception.

But the mansion itself was very impressive. It was twice the size of any earthlodge of Sheheke's era. It sat apart from the other homes and shops in the young republic's even younger capital. The month of Little Cold was giving way to real winter, the month of the Seven Cold Days, back home on the Northern Plains, but in Washington the weather was more like the month known to Sheheke as the Breaking Up of the Ice.

Sheheke had spent three months traveling through American cities and countryside. Vast stretches of the country he had seen were thinly populated by white men and many Indian nations still filled the enormous space between St. Louis and Washington, but it was clear that these Americans had control over that territory. The party had traveled without much concern for self-defense. He'd seen

dozens of towns, hundreds of independent farmsteads and planta-
tions, trading posts, stores, and inns. The United States was a nation
on a wholly different scale than anything with which Sheheke was
familiar. In Sheheke's lifetime it had never taken more than part of a
day to ride the entire length of Mandan country, that is, from On-a-
Slant on the south and west to the Larson site on the north and
east. Mandan hunting territory and the area from which the
Mandan drew resources was much larger than that, of course, but
all of that turf away from the Missouri and beyond the villages was
contested. It was safer to travel the 1,600 miles from St. Louis to
Washington than to ride 100 miles from the Knife River metropolitan area to the Bad Lands.

His culture shock at total immersion into the Americans' world
could only be increasing. As he spent time in the heart of the
Americans' huge land, he must have become disturbingly aware of
their power. Sheheke knew, after his months among them, that his
own nation had no very attractive alternative to befriending the
Americans. The distance from their centers of power would make it
difficult for them to prosecute a war on the Upper Missouri, but it
was clearly not impossible. They were already well-established on the
river to the south. It was the Americans who sent an expedition to
the Mandan cities and forced their passage twice through hostile
territory, not the other way around.

Whatever doubts he may have harbored about the wisdom of
going on this diplomatic mission must have vanished as he gained
first-hand knowledge of the power of the Americans. The Spanish
were gone, their Welsh, French, and Scottish representatives now swal-
lowed up in the new American nation. The French themselves may
have been strong once, but they were now largely powerless on the
continent. They had traders—bold, independent, and tough men—but
no armies. The English were an alternative, and they had some forts
on the Northern Plains, but the British had always been closer to the
Hidatsa and, too, Sheheke had never seen their cities, their leaders, or
their military might. They never came to his villages with a force like
the Americans had mounted. He had seen enough of the Americans
to understand that they would make better friends than enemies.

Thomas Jefferson was clearly excited to meet the man he called Wolf, and that attitude was likely infectious. The men apparently hit it off, Sheheke deciding that the Great Father was worthy of being called a brother. Well-mannered Thomas Jefferson would have inquired as to whether the chief's party had found itself welcome in the United States and as to the comfort of the accommodations. The Great White Coyote certainly brought greetings on behalf of his people and proclaimed his pleasure at meeting the leader of his great nation. He probably expressed a hope that the United States and the Mandan Nation would always be friends and would become good trading partners.

The President then broadened his welcome and his oratory to Sheheke's delegation. He delivered a speech, one very much like the speeches he typically gave to Indian leaders:

> I take you by the hand of friendship hearty welcome to the seat of the government of the United States. The journey which you have taken to visit your fathers on this side of our island is a long one, and your having undertaken it is a proof that you desired to become acquainted with us. I thank the Great Spirit that he has protected you through the journey and brought you safely to the residence of your friends, and I hope He will have you constantly in his safe keeping, and restore you in good health to your nations and families.[81]

Sheheke, his English improved by spending four months in almost total immersion in the language, would have understood some words, at least, but it seems he still needed an interpreter to follow Jefferson's meaning. The idea that his entire world was an island must have been an interesting and slightly disturbing concept. Sheheke knew though, from long experience and from taking an interest in other cultures, that different nations had vastly different stories of their origin. The Ojibwa, for instance, believed that the world rested on the back of a giant turtle. Jefferson went on to talk about his nation's theories.

> My friends and children, we are descended from
> the old nations which live beyond the great water,
> but we and our forefathers have been so long here
> that we seem like you to have grown out of this
> land. We consider ourselves no longer of the old
> nations beyond the great water, but as united in one
> family with our red brethren here. The French, the
> English, the Spaniards, have now agreed with us to
> retire from all the country which you and we hold
> between Canada and Mexico, and never more to
> return to it. And remember the words I now speak
> to you, my children, they are never to return again.

Bold talk, but Sheheke could believe some of it might be true.
The French-speaking traders at the villages were there at the suffer-
ance of the English companies doing business with the Mandan and
Hidatsa. The Spaniards hadn't been around since Evans and it had
been explained to Sheheke that the United States had taken over
their lands on the Lower Missouri. The English, however, showed no
signs of leaving. They had prospered after the Spanish proclamations
and even as President Jefferson addressed him, Sheheke could have
every confidence that at that very moment some Canadian trader
was dining in a lodge at Mitutanka. He'd heard before that the
Mandan were supposed to turn away from their old trading partners
to the north. The Mandan, though, were free traders. The idea that
there was an authority that could restrict trade was ridiculous.

The President continued,

> As soon as Spain had agreed to withdraw from all
> the waters of the Missouri and Mississippi, I felt the
> desire of becoming acquainted with all my red chil-
> dren beyond the Mississippi, and of uniting them
> with us as we have those on this side of that river, in
> the bonds of peace and friendship. I wished to learn
> what we could do to benefit them by furnishing

them the necessaries they want in exchange for their furs and peltries.

I have therefore sent our beloved man, Captain Lewis, one of my own family, to go up the Missouri river to get acquainted with all the Indian nations in its neighborhood, to take them by the hand, deliver my talks to them, and to inform us in what way we could be useful to them. Your nation received him kindly, you have taken him by the hand and been friendly to him. My children, I thank you for the services you rendered him, and for your attention to his words. He will now tell us where we should establish trading houses to be convenient to you all, and what we must send to them.

My friends and children, I have now important advice to give you. I have already told you that you and all the red men are my children, and I wish you to live in peace and friendship with one another as brethren of the same family ought to do. How much better it is for neighbors to help than to hurt one another; how much happier must it make them.

If you will cease to make war on one another, if you will live in friendship with all mankind, you can employ all your time in providing food and clothing for yourselves and your families. Your men will not be destroyed in war, and your women and children will lie down to sleep in their cabins without fear of being surprised by their enemies and killed or carried away. Your numbers will increase instead of diminishing, and you will live in plenty and in quiet.

The Wolf in Washington

Coyote agreed with what the President was saying. It was, after all, Mandan policy.

Jefferson went on,

My children, I have given this advice to all your red brethren on this side of the Mississippi; they are following it, they are increasing in their numbers, are learning to clothe and provide for their families as we do. Remember then my advice, my friend; carry it home to your people, and tell them that from the day that they become all of the same family, from the day that we become father to them all, we wish, as a true father should do, that we may all live together as one household, and that before they strike one another, they should to their father and let him endeavor to make up the quarrel.

My children, you are come from the other side of our great island, from where the sun sets, to see your new friends at the sun rising. You have now arrived where the waters are constantly rising and falling every day, but you are still distant from the sea. I very much desire that you should not stop here, but go and see your brethren as far as the edge of the great water. I am persuaded you have so far seen that every man by the way has received you as his brothers, and has been ready to do you all the kindness in his power. You will see the same thing quite to the sea shore; and I wish you, therefore, to go and visit our great cities in that quarter, and see how many friends and brothers you have here. You will then have traveled a long line from west to east, and if you had time to go from north to south, from Canada to Florida, you would find it as long in that direction, and all the people as sincerely your friends. I invite you, therefore, to pay a visit to

Baltimore, Philadelphia, New York, and the cities
still beyond that, if you are willing to go further.

We will provide carriages to convey you and a person to go with you to see that you want for nothing.
By the time you come back the snows will be melted
on the mountains, the ice in the rivers broken up, and
you will be wishing to set out on your return home.

My children, I have long desired to see you;
I have now opened my heart to you, let my words
sink into your hearts and never be forgotten. If ever
lying people or bad spirits should raise up clouds
between us, call to mind what I have said, and what
you have seen yourselves. Be sure there are some
lying spirits between us.

Would that be the Lakota he was referring to, Sheheke may have
wondered, or was he admitting that he could not control all of his
people any more than an Indian chief could keep his young men
from sometimes causing mischief? Either way, his next words, were
appropriate, if idealistic.

Let us come together as friends and explain to
each other what is misrepresented or misunderstood,
the clouds will fly away like morning fog, and the
sun of friendship appear and shine forever bright
and clear between us.

My children, it may happen that while you are
here occasion may arise to talk about many things
which I do not now particularly mention. The
Secretary of War will always be ready to talk with
you, and you are to consider whatever he says as said
by myself. He will also take care of you and see that
you are furnished with all comforts here.

If Sheheke commented on Jefferson's speech, the words are lost now. Being a diplomat, he probably wouldn't have said all that he thought, anyway. The practical problems of the President's high-sounding plan were many.

Nations have reasons, good or bad, for going to war. The Ojibwa people moved west at the frontier of French exploration. Their move pressured the Dakota and Lakota, forcing a long-running war to control the resources of the rice and buffalo of the Minnesota lakes and prairies. The Lakota moved to the Missouri and pressured the nations already there, seizing the buffalo-hunting territory and sometimes the crops or scalps of nations that had been fighting among themselves, on and off, for at least four hundred years. Getting all those nations to quit warring would be a remarkable diplomatic achievement. Throw in the Crow, Cheyenne, Blackfoot, Assiniboine, and all the other bands and tribes and it was nearly impossible to even imagine.

Then there was the problem of distance. Jefferson was right in suggesting that direct conversation between leaders was an effective antidote for the poison of misunderstanding and misrepresentation. But a four-month trip separated Mitutanka from Washington. It made Jefferson's observation pointless. A lot of damage could be done in the eight months it would take for the sun to chase away the fog of deceit. It was Mandan tradition that the geographical relationship between peoples was important in maintaining good relations. That was the essence of an old Mandan story about the arrival of one of the bands of Hidatsa on the Missouri. Alfred Bowers recounted the story of one Mandan elder telling the Hidatsa to go north with their villages:

> It would be better if you went upstream and built
> your own village for our customs are somewhat dif-
> ferent from yours. Not knowing each other's ways
> the young men might have differences and then
> there would be wars. Do not go too far away for
> people who live far apart are like strangers and wars
> break out between them. Travel north only until you

cannot see the smoke from our lodges and there
build your village. Then we will be close enough to
be friends and not far enough away to be enemies.[82]

It would be surprising if a veteran diplomat like Sheheke did not
see a contradiction between the words and the desires of American
policy. It was his clear understanding, based on many fireside talks
with the two Captains and their eagerness in the winter of 1804–05
to carry punitive expeditions against the Lakota, that the United
States wanted the Indian nations to unite against the Lakota people.
It was a desire he shared, if peace could not be assured another way.

One comment the President made told Sheheke something
about the system of leadership the Americans employed. There was a
war leader, apparently, because Jefferson had delegated responsibility
to the Secretary of War, but that leading warrior was not the "Great
Father." In the United States, as in Mitutanka, the peace chief was
apparently supreme.

Sheheke made more of a stir in Washington than he had in the
frontier city of St. Louis. Deputations of Indian chiefs were not
unique in the young nation's capital. Chiefs from west of the
Mississippi, however, were rare as could be. The only previous visitor
from Sheheke's neighborhood, the Arikara Arketarnawhar (Is-a-
Whippoorwill) had died during his visit in early 1806. So, when the
family group, Sheheke, Yellow Corn, and their son, extended with
the Jessaumes, made a public appearance, they drew a lot of attention. Sheheke was, in fact, subject of a newspaper notice promoting
his participation in a "Grand Indian Dance" during the final night
performance of an acrobatic troupe at the theatre.

On New Year's Day, the Indian party from the Upper Missouri
was taken by Meriwether Lewis to a theatre, The Theatre, in fact. It
had been announced in the December 31, 1806, edition of the
National Intelligencer: "AT THE THEATRE ON THURSDAY
EVENING, JAN 1: . . . GRAND INDIAN DANCE IN CHAR-
ACTER. The Chief of the Mandans, and Osage Indians will dance
several dances of character and the great Calumet Dance, which has
never been performed before." Sheheke and Yellow Corn started the

night in the audience, though, not on stage. Yellow Corn was striking. She wore many earrings. Her hair was parted in the middle,
showing the red line tattooed back from her forehead. She wore
no paint on her face. Augustus John Foster described her as having
pretty features and skin of a pale, yellowish hue.[83] He was surprised
to learn that the Mandan chief was monogamous, as that was not his
stereotype of Indian people.[84]

The international show began with "A Spanish Dance by the
Little American," who danced on a tight rope.[85] More acrobatics and
aerial dances followed. Miss Louisa performed a dance "in character," using a balance pole. Miss Catherine followed with an Italian
dance, finishing her first appearance on stage with what the newspaper called a "ferious dance." The Manfredis, Madam and Mister, then
took the stage. Madam somehow danced "without putting her feet
on the rope," and also played the mandolin while in the air. Her
husband gave a Cossack performance and danced on the rope with
a boy on his shoulders. It seems ironic, as seen from the twenty-first
century when Indian hoop dancers frequently astound white audi-
ences, that Mr. Manfredi put on a hoop dance for the Indians and
other spectators. He presented then a feature called "Grand Military
Evolutions, etc." It may have been his "Drunken Dragoon" act, or
perhaps it was the "numerous comic capers" of the clown, who
played against the acrobats, diverting them with pratfalls, but at some
point, the spectacle tickled the folks from the Upper Missouri.
Yellow Corn and Jessaume's wife both laughed hysterically. Unsure,
however, if it would be impolite for him to laugh, the chief pulled
at his cheeks and chin trying, in vain, to avoid outright guffaws.

Tumbling children, bouncing across the carpet in the "Italian
style," threw somersaults, "backward and forward over tables and
chairs—ground tumbling, with English and Spanish dances."
Harkening back to ancient Mediterranean entertainments, Mr.
Manfredi balanced several persons on his arms, legs and trunk, in a
sequence called "The Egyptian Pyramids," during which he showed
"several perspectives in the Roman style." Manfredi concluded that
portion of the act with a fandango stepped off around several eggs.

The Indians were eventually invited to the stage. The Great

White Coyote was given a throne, befitting the man being called a "Mandan King." The Osage danced while Sheheke respectfully observed and portrayed a quiet dignity.

Mr. Manfredi and Catherine reappeared, dressed as Indians, and the evening concluded with the two of them in a "Grand Combat with Sabers."

Two weeks later, January 14, a dinner was presented in honor of Captain Lewis, Clark having not yet arrived in the District of Columbia. The party was delayed for several days to allow Clark time to share in the recognition, but was finally held without him. Clark showed up a week later. Washington Mayor Robert Brent presided over an assemblage including several members of Congress and government officials. The group from St. Louis was well-represented. Pierre Chouteau, Pierre Provenchere, and Sheheke attended. An elegant dinner, with a festive board, according to the *Universal Gazette*, was given by the citizens of Washington imbued with a sense of gratitude for Captain Lewis. After dinner, Sheheke heard again a series of toasts offered to the two leaders of the group that had come to his village twenty-six months earlier. There were, again, seventeen toasts raised before Lewis was excused. They were properly interspersed with appropriate songs and instrumental music.[86] The content of the brief speeches echoed some of the sentiments heard in St. Louis, but among the Washingtonians, there was a more pronounced wish to involve Sheheke and his people in the toasts. Three of the seventeen spoke directly to Native American ears.[87]

"The United States—Who, by respecting the rights of her native children, has inspired them with reverence for her power, and affection for her laws," started the Indian series. "The Red People of America—Under an enlightened policy, gaining by steady steps the comforts of the civilized, without losing the virtues of the savage state," was followed by, "The Council Fire—May it long continue to diffuse a genial warmth, without consuming those who surround it."

It was at this party that Lewis expressed a brief but deep philosophical sentiment, apparently on his mind since his return as a conquering deed-doer to the seat of political talk in the United States: "May works be a test of patriotism, as they ought of right to be that of religion."

Sheheke visited Philadelphia sometime between January 15 and February 10. The nation's first capital was the largest city in America with a population of 30,000, a single city six times bigger than the combined population of all five Knife River villages. It was probably in Philadelphia that Sheheke and Yellow Corn both sat for the noted portraitist Charles Balthazar Julien Fevret de St. Memin. The timing would be right for him to be with the group of Indians who left Philadelphia on February 10, some of whom were "sadly deseased," according to Charles Wilson Peale.[88] A group Peale identified to Jefferson as "the Indians," had been visiting "the women of bad fame in the lower part of the town and contracted the venerial disease." Peale admitted that he had only heard this story and had not attempted to verify it, but thought it was his duty to alert Jefferson so that the President could order steps taken to cure the condition "before their departure."

It's likely Sheheke visited Baltimore and New York, as invited to do by President Jefferson. He would have seen harbors on the Atlantic, filled with ships that would dwarf the keelboat that had appeared so impressive on the Upper Missouri. He saw, in a country still in its infancy, a widespread use of construction techniques undreamed of by the women of Mitutanka. He saw carriages, wagons, horses, and people—thousands, tens of thousands, of people. The Mandan chief was undoubtedly shown examples of American art, sculpture, and paintings. He noted in widespread use, as household goods, manufac-tured items never seen on the Upper Missouri. He dined at tables, sat in chairs, and walked and stood in buildings with polished wood and even marble floors in place of the hard-packed earth of Mitutanka's lodges. He saw countless wonders. He accumulated stories.

Outside of his few days in the limelight in the Capital City, Sheheke seems to have traveled almost incognito in the East. Newspapers in New York and Philadelphia, at least those that have survived, took no notice of his visits. He moved through the heart of the United States quietly, gaining material for a lifetime of story-telling in the earthlodges of home. About ten weeks after he had entered Washington, it was time to head home.

9

Ensign Pryor's Fight

Compared to the first effort—the organization of the Lewis and Clark Corps of Discovery—not nearly so much care went into planning the second United States expedition to the Mandan Indians. The dam had broken, or so it seemed to American policy makers.

On March 9, 1807, Secretary of War Henry Dearborn issued orders to William Clark, Colonel Thomas Hunt, and former Sergeant, now Ensign, Nathaniel Pryor. The orders directed the men to arrange for the return of Chief Sheheke and his family to his village. Hunt, still the commandant of Camp Bellefontaine near St. Louis, was told to give Pryor the services of "one careful, sober serjeant and ten good sober privates" to accompany Sheheke on his return. In a packet containing Clark's $1,500 per year commission as the "Agent of Indian Affairs to the Several Nations of Indians within the Territory of Louisiana excepting the Great and little Osages and their several divisions, and detachments," Dearborn also included the orders for Hunt and Clark, authorizing Clark to allow Ensign Pryor to add up to six men to that squad if he was able to recruit appropriate men to his service. Pryor found several others who were willing to enlist in the cause.

Dearborn anticipated a desire on the part of St. Louis merchants to take advantage of the military escort. If they could act without delay, Dearborn wrote, Clark could grant them leave to send a suitable number of men and amount of goods "to trade with the Indians generally on the Missouri from the Ricaras upward." Their trading licenses would be monopolies for two years at least. Further, the United States would subsidize the traders with ammunition, "say two pounds of powder, and lead or ball in proportion, to each man."[89]

Delays did happen, but Clark excused each of them for cause. On May 18, he wrote to Dearborn announcing that Pryor's party would consist of Pryor, fourteen soldiers, and the scion of fur trade king Pierre Chouteau, the young August Chouteau with twenty-two men in his employ. Chouteau was to establish trading relations with the Mandan. They would be leaving that very evening, Clark wrote. But the trip did not immediately get under way. Some Sioux came to town, chiefs and warriors of "considerable note."[90] This changed the plan.

On June 1, Clark wrote to Dearborn informing him that the Sioux, who he had previously referenced as representatives of the "most numerous and vicious bands" along the Missouri, had been greatly mollified and highly pleased with their reception in St. Louis. Pierre Chouteau had seen to it that they enjoyed themselves. Sheheke suggested that the trip home might go more smoothly if the party from the United States was accompanied by the Sioux. This seemed like a good stratagem, especially as it was advanced by the veteran Mandan diplomat. Hospitality meant safety on the Northern Plains. Traveling with highly pleased Sioux warriors would facilitate an easier passage through the most dangerous territory between him and his earthlodge, he believed. Traveling and camping together might even allow time for discussions of peace between the Sioux and the Mandan. Past personal relationships more than once meant the difference between life and death in chance meetings of warriors. The fellowship might be useful and, in any event, could do no harm. Clark endorsed the idea.

Colonel Hunt committed another officer, a Lieutenant, and seven more soldiers and boatmen to accompany the Sioux. This brought the whole force to either 102 or 108 people: Lieutenant Joseph Kimble; Ensign Pryor; a sergeant (presumably sober); a corporal; eighteen privates; and four civilian employees of the government to hunt and keep a boat afloat. August Chouteau also had a boat and a pirogue and thirty-two men. Trader Pierre Dorian, who had brought the Sioux to St. Louis, was also along. He had a boat and ten men. There were eighteen Indian men, eight women, and six children. It's not clear where or whether Sheheke, Yellow Corn, Jessaume, and the rest of their families fit into that roster.

The party left St. Louis and headed north. It was expected that, after the Sioux were returned to their people, Kimble would return to Bellefontaine. Pryor's party would then consist of forty-eight men, "which will be fully sufficient," Clark wrote, "to pass any hostile band which he may probably meet with."[91]

Clark's view of the political situation on the Upper Missouri was simplistic. He believed that the earthlodge peoples were bullied and harassed by the nomadic tribes. In the case of the Mandan, he felt they were under constant pressure from the Assiniboine and Lakota, which was not far from the truth, but an analysis that still doesn't take into account the long-standing trading relationship between the Mandan and Assiniboine. The Assiniboine had been the first, and over time had been more reliable deliverers of white goods than the various white factions had been themselves. In the case of the Arikara, Clark viewed the various bands generally called Sioux as bullies who dominated the Arikara and forced the peaceful farming people to sometimes do things contrary to their own nature and certainly contrary to the wishes of the United States. But while the Arikara and Mandan certainly felt pressure from their nomadic neighbors, the idea that their relationships with these peoples were totally one-sided was far from true. Having that naive perspective, Clark presumed that any trouble for Pryor would come from independent war parties, not from a concerted national effort to prevent his passage.

But on the morning of September 9, 1807, that is exactly what confronted Pryor and Sheheke. Pulling upriver along the east bank, the boats came in sight of the lower Arikara village, which lay on the west bank below the mouth of the Grand River. As they came opposite the village, they heard guns fired and noted several shots plunking into the river near their boats. Pierre Dorian called out in the Siouan tongue, asking the meaning of the gunfire.

"Put to shore," he was answered. "We will supply you with corn and oil."

Ensign Pryor had been with these people twice before and in many somewhat similar circumstances in other places on the Lewis and Clark expedition. He determined that showing confidence in the Arikara offer was the best move. He didn't know that they were angry at both the United States and the Mandans. Pryor steered the boats to the west bank. A group of Sioux came to the beach to meet them, telling Dorian that the Mandan and the Arikara were now at war. Two Arikara had recently been killed by Mandans at the Cannonball River. Their anger at the United States was perhaps even greater. Pryor, or his superiors, knew that could be the case.

Before Sheheke went to Washington, an Arikara chief had accepted an invitation to visit the President. Arketarnawhar Was-to-ne, Is-a-Whippoorwill, made it to Washington, Baltimore, and Philadelphia in 1806. It had not been an easy trip. He traveled down to St. Louis with the keelboat in the spring of 1805, but there found himself stricken ill along with several other Indians making up a deputation to Washington. Ascribing the illness to being away from their homes, several demanded to go back upriver, with a soldierly escort, because they feared the Sioux and other Indian nations. A very small escort was provided by St. Louis area military commander and Spanish secret agent James Wilkinson, it being deemed improper to force the chiefs to continue their trip against their will. The escort was not large enough. On the way upriver in late-1805, the Kansas Indians opposed the mission and Was-to-ne found himself back in St. Louis. He then agreed to let Wilkinson send him on to Washington.

Once there, in early 1806, the President took him by the hand "with affection," according to Jefferson.[92] Secretary of War Henry Dearborn found him to be an interesting character. The Arikara traveled in the East, as Sheheke would later, with a group of other Indians, seven in all. While in Washington they were in the care of innkeeper Lewis Morin. He was to see to their needs in Washington and arrange their transportation to Pittsburgh.[93]

Unfortunately for international relations, the Arikara chief died in Washington on April 7.[94] Dearborn and Jefferson realized that this meant trouble for government policy. Dearborn assigned trader Joseph Gravelines to go to the Arikara to break the news. He was to take with him a Pawnee who spoke Arikara and they were to take plenty of presents, compensation for the death of the chief. Gifts of goods worth two or three hundred dollars were to be distributed to his wives and children. His clothes, medicine bag and other belongings, and the presidential peace medal the Arketarnawhar had been given were packaged for his favorite son. Gravelines was also given powder and lead to hand out to Arikara and Mandan chiefs. He would also serve as a mailman.

President Jefferson wrote two letters for Gravelines to carry to the Upper Missouri—a letter of sympathy and hope for friendship for the Arikara and an invitation to Mandan chiefs to come for a visit. Jefferson seems not to have seen the irony in his own gentle chastisement in the letter to the "chiefs & people of the Mandane nation," when he wrote, "I should have recieved with great satisfaction . . . some of your chiefs, with those of the Osages, Ricaras, Missouris, Panis & others who have lately visited us." He wrote the letter to the Mandan on the same day he gave a death notice to the Arikara. To make matters worse, the Arikara was not the only one not coming home from his trip to the nation's capital; six of the seven chiefs entrusted to Morin died in his care. He billed the government for funeral expenses. Jefferson did not let on to the Mandan that if they had sent their chiefs they more than likely would be dead.

Jefferson's letter to the Arikara explained that their Arketarnawhar had taken ill in Washington where everything possible had been done to help him, "but it pleased the great Spirit to take him from among us. We buried him among our own deceased friends and relatives, we shed many tears over his grave. . . . But death must happen to all men, and his time was come." The President used the opportunity to tell the Arikara that their departed chief had brought assurances of their friendship and had pledged that the Arikara and the Americans would become one family.

The message was dead on arrival. The messenger may have been, too, except for his previous experience with the Arikara and the presents he handed out. Before he was allowed to leave, Gravelines was roughed up by angry Arikara when he brought word of the Arketarnawhar's death to their villages in the summer of 1807.

Manuel Lisa walked into the same trouble shortly after. Lisa was already on Ensign Pryor's bad side when he paddled into Arikara country ahead of the mission to return Sheheke. Lisa had been told, at St. Charles in the spring, to wait and accompany Pryor to the Mandan. He had agreed, according to Pryor,[95] but then missed the rendezvous and raced ahead of the government-sponsored expedition.

When he reached the Arikara in August, Lisa found them riled up. He avoided serious trouble by giving up some guns and by deflecting the Arikara anger toward the oncoming party. Lisa told the Indians that two boats would soon be coming, both filled with trade goods and one carrying a Mandan chief. To help effect his escape, Lisa told them that the boats that were coming were intended completely for the Arikara trade.

As Pryor landed, a captive Mandan woman made her way through a crowd of armed warriors on the beach. Pryor admitted her on board, and she filled him in on the Lisa incident and the plans the Arikara had for Pryor's party. They had determined in council, she said, to kill Lisa and seize the rest of his goods upon his return and had laid plans for the murder and plunder of the Mandan chief and his entourage. Pryor's own senses told him there was trouble in the air; he could see the Arikara and their Sioux allies "checking their bullets and driving away their women and children."

Ensign Pryor ordered Sheheke to secure himself in the boat's cabin. A breastwork was erected by piling trunks and boxes in front of the cabin. Then he went to talk with an old friend.

Clark had asked Pryor to give a peace medal to a particular

Arikara chief named Grey Eyes, who was known to have great influence and was thought to be friendly to the United States. Grey Eyes came to Pryor bringing a letter from another white trader who wrote that he had been roughed up by the Arikara. The chief expressed his good wishes for Sheheke and the party, but he was clearly uncomfortable. A council was reluctantly agreed to through the exertions of Dorian. Many of the chiefs attended, but not the most significant leader of the upper village. Peace reigned, briefly, but Pryor worried. If fruitless talks continued too long, they risked the danger of becoming easy prey to mischief at nightfall.

Pryor thought it incumbent upon himself to deliver a speech, which he did, through a translator, a Spaniard in whom he had no confidence. His speech, as he remembered it, was very respectful of the Arikara and reminded them of the bond of friendship forged by Lewis and Clark's trips through their country in the previous three years. It also tried to remind them of the Native American tradition of hospitality so common on the Northern Plains.

> Your Great American Father has sent me with a few of his soldiers to conduct the Mandane chief to his nation. In our long and laborious journey, we have met with many nations of red People, by all of whom we have been treated with hospitality and kindness. I have repeated to them that talk of their Great Father, whose counsels they will in future pursue. We are not strangers to you: On a former occasion you extended to Louis and Clark the hand of friendship. We feasted in your villages and exchanged mutual benefit. As a proof of the confidence of your Great Father in a continuance of your pacific dispositions, and as an evidence of his personal friendship for your chief, he sends him a large Medal the devices of which may continually remind you of the amicable intercourse which ought always subsist between his People and yours.

At the end of his speech, Pryor put the medal around the neck of Chief Grey Eyes. The Pryor expedition continued upriver after promising to visit the upper village. Jessaume and Dorian were, in effect, hostages, as they walked in a mob to the other village. Threatening warriors walked along the shore and above the bank, joining others to make a large angry crowd on the beach by the time the Pryor and Chouteau boats reached the second village. Though it may have been the most sensible course, they couldn't just break their promise and pass the village on the opposite side of the river. Jessaume and Dorian would be left in serious trouble.

It was about four in the afternoon when the Americans landed just below the second Arikara village. There were 650 warriors on the beach in a "violent rage." The soldiers were ready. When the Arikara pointed toward a narrow channel, urging Pryor's boats into it, Pryor declined. There was no doubt that trouble lay up the channel. But rather than lay offshore on a sandbar, he took his boats right onto the crowded beach. Pryor reported to Clark that he felt at that time that if an attack came, "it was doubtless, as prudent to meet it on the beach as to be followed into a river filled with irregular Sand Bars."

There was a nasty conversation on the beach. They could go no farther, the Arikara said. They had been told by Lisa that all the goods on those two boats were meant for them. Pryor's boat held the soldiers and Sheheke; Chouteau's barge held the fur traders and boatmen. The Arikara grabbed the cable of Chouteau's boat and made as if to appropriate it. They waved to Pryor then, telling him he could go. That was an important moment. If Pryor had taken the Arikara at their word and cast off with his soldiers and his Mandan chief, they would have very likely completed the assigned mission on time and without casualties.

Chouteau pleaded with Pryor not to abandon him to the hostile crowd. Pryor told Chouteau to make a deal; he probably pointed out that since he was a trader, he should make a trade. Chouteau tried, but the price was already going too high, Pryor could see. "He at length did make them an offer, which, had they not been determined on plunder and blood, ought to have satisfied them."

Chouteau was still negotiating, though; he only offered half his goods, and those for trade, not for presents. He would leave a man with the Arikara, to carry out the trade. The chief of the upper village boarded Pryor's boat and made it clear that he wanted Sheheke to go on shore with him. Pryor refused and the chief departed.

The demands of the Arikara reached their peak. They wanted all of Chouteau's guns and ammunition and they were going to take it. Grey Eyes ripped the peace medal from his neck and threw it to the ground. One of Chouteau's men was knocked down with the butt end of a gun. The warriors ran from the beach, firing as they retired into a willow thicket. Pryor's men did not hesitate. Even before the Indians could reach relative safety, a directed volley of swivel cannon, blunderbusses and small arms fire cut into them. A Hunkpapa Lakota named *Oglesa*, or Red Shirt, was killed in the crossfire.[96] Rene Jessaume was also wounded in the initial action. He took two bullets. Even so, he recovered the peace medal and fired off more than forty shots at the Arikara.

The fight settled into a fixed battle at thirty to sixty yards. The Indians were better concealed, and the Americans better armed, but vastly outnumbered. After fifteen minutes, Pryor had seen enough. He ordered a retreat to the boats and had them cast off with the current. Pryor's craft slipped into the current easily, but Chouteau was hung up on a sandbar. His men had to expose themselves to set the boat back into the current. They took casualties.

The two boats floated with the rapid current downriver, carrying on a battle with warriors on both sides of the river for about an hour. Finally, shortly before sunset, the Americans saw a group of forty Indians trying to get to a point projecting out into the river before the boats could pass it. They were led by a Sioux warrior who had been on Pryor's boat and was known to him by the white bandage he wore around his head. He was targeted by Pryor's sharpshooters and killed. His associates broke off their attack.

A short time later, feeling safer, Pryor and Chouteau lashed their boats together and counted the wounded. Chouteau had lost one man dead on the beach, another in a pirogue, and one on his boat. A fourth man was mortally wounded. Chouteau had six other wounded, including Rene Jessaume. Pryor had three wounded, two soldiers and his hunter, George Shannon. Shannon, who had been part of the Lewis and Clark Expedition, had his leg broken. He lost it. Later, as "Peg Leg" Shannon, he won a seat in Congress from his home state of Kentucky.[97]

Pryor had a mission, and though this had clearly been a serious and unforeseen difficulty for which he could not be blamed, still he considered other ways to accomplish the goal. He approached Sheheke about making an overland trek to the Mandan villages, avoiding the Arikara towns along the Missouri. Pryor thought it might be as easy as a three-day walk. Sheheke refused to consider it, not wanting to travel overland with the women and children and a wounded Jessaume.

Jessaume was amazed that the casualty total wasn't higher. "I am still unable to understand how amid seven hundred Indians, almost all armed, firing at Mr. Chouteau's barge where I was, and only thirty paces away, we had only four men killed and five wounded."[98] As one who had tried to prevent the fight as an interpreter and full-time village resident, Jessaume was sure as to the cause: "The Ricaras are jealous of the return of the Mandan chief, and wish to kill him," he wrote to President Jefferson in December.

Pryor had no choice. He let the Missouri carry him to St. Louis. Sheheke would not make it home in 1807. If he was ever going to make it home against Arikara opposition, Pryor believed that it would take an army. Less than four hundred men should not even attempt it, he told Clark, and a thousand soldiers might fail in the mission.[99]

10

Exiled in St. Louis

No one, Sheheke included, had expected that he would be back in St. Louis for a third time before 1807 was out. But there he was, a guest of the United States, and neither the guest nor the host was particularly happy about it.

While Pryor's expedition was getting organized in the spring of 1807, Sheheke and his family were put up at Cantonment Bellefontaine. Sheheke was treated in a manner befitting his status as a visiting dignitary, that is, he ate with the officers. The cantonment, unfortunately, had little to recommend it as a resort.

The United States' first fort west of the Mississippi, Cantonment Bellefontaine was created while Lewis and Clark were struggling across the Rockies on their way west. It was north of St. Louis, east of St. Charles, and just west of the confluence of the mighty Missouri with its kid brother, the Mississippi. Cold Water Creek rolled by the site. What had suggested it as a fort site may have been the beautiful spring that gave the cantonment its name.[100] It turned out to be a bad location, however.

The territorial governor and General James Wilkinson didn't think the heights above the river would be sufficiently convenient to water and lumber. He preferred the wooded bottoms at the joining of Cold Water Creek and the Missouri River. Not everyone agreed with that preference. One officer was quoted in 1807 as having previously said that the American soldiers "were encamped on a low damp bottom subject to be overflowed." It overflowed regularly. Initially the dampness was a bother, an inconvenience in the construction of the fort. Later it became a safety hazard and, finally, the water swept the field entirely.

The fort consisted of a series of huts, each crowded with about fifteen soldiers, officers' quarters, a blacksmith's shop, quartermaster's storehouse, laboratory, magazine, contractor's store, and the commanding officer's quarters. It was built in the summer and fall of 1805. On October 29 of that year Colonel Thomas Hunt took command of the post. Hunt was a Revolutionary War veteran, having joined as a boy, a private "centinel" who soldiered through the war and retired in 1783 as a captain. Civilian life didn't hold him long when word reached him that General "Mad Anthony" Wayne was staffing a western expedition. As a frontier veteran, Hunt was the first commandant of Bellefontaine, and it was his last assignment.

When Sheheke first arrived at the cantonment with Lewis and Clark in September 1806, it was Hunt who ordered the cannons fired in honor of the expedition. At that time, Sergeant Ordway described it as a handsome establishment.

Hunt was still there when Sheheke returned in the spring of 1807. The fort may not have changed a great deal by that time, and Sheheke was treated by the commanding officer as an honored guest. But the fort, by the time his St. Louis exile ended in 1809, had surely become an inadequate home for a leading family of the Northern Plains. The place was falling down.

Colonel Hunt was once again Sheheke's host after Ensign Pryor's defeat at the Arikara villages, but only until August 18, 1808, the day Hunt died. The succeeding commanding officer did not arrive at Cantonment Bellefontaine until May 20, 1809.[101] What Lieutenant Colonel Daniel Bissell found then was a mess. He immediately appointed a board of officers to inspect all the fort's buildings. Their report was damning. The buildings were decayed and dangerous. They were unhealthy for a multitude of reasons, not the least of which was that they could fall down on their inhabitants. Should they remain standing, they were still nasty from dampness and rot. Most of the buildings, including all of the inhabited ones, were decayed. They had been built without foundations. Logs rested on the ground. The men's huts were thrown together with bark on green wood, and so decayed easily. The officers' quarters were the same and even the commanding officer's quarters was built with logs in contact with wet earth. It was all "rotten, damp and unwholesome," in the words of the investigating officers' report.

Sheheke let it be known that he would prefer to wait in St. Louis for the next attempt to return him home. Frederick Bates, the acting governor of Louisiana during Meriwether Lewis' absence, expressed frustration with Sheheke's attitude in a letter to George Rogers Clark:

> The Mandane Chief heretofore happy at the camp, where I have always seen him at the Officers tables, and treated with every kind and hospitable indulgence now insists on being at St. Louis. He is made to believe that he is the 'Brother' and not the 'Son' of the President, that this is the residence of Gov. Lewis and yourself and is (resolved) so, that while you were here, he was not sent among the 'Little Chiefs' at the camp.
>
> How trifling and vexatious! A false sensibility is excited and his mind poisoned by the mischievous suggestions. I am indirectly told that P. Chouteau provides for him since his abrupt return from Belle Fontaine.[102]

In St. Louis, the Chouteau family lived in an impressive style. Patriarch Auguste Chouteau's home was described as "an elegant domicile fronting on Main Street. His dwelling and houses for his servants occupied the whole square. . . . The walls were two and a half feet thick, of solid stone work, two stories high and surrounded by a large piazza. The floors were of black walnut, and were polished so finely that they reflected like a mirror."[103]

It appears that Pierre Chouteau acted to improve Sheheke's living conditions in exile. What improvement there was, whether to a room in one of his family's homes or to guest or servants' quarters, and whether or not Chouteau's hospitality lasted an entire year and a half is unclear. What is clear is that the issue was important enough to Sheheke that he risked for its sake abusing his relationship with a fairly significant American official. The Mandan chief who had visited the home of, and had been the guest of, the President of the United States was not content with damp and moldy quarters for himself and his family. This was the sole occasion in Sheheke's relationship with the United States where he expressed dissatisfaction with the Americans.

The year 1808 played out, with the Americans becoming ever more embarrassed by their inability to deliver, literally and figuratively, for the Mandan. Sheheke and his family waited.

With 1809 came hope for another attempt.

11

The Honor of the United States

From the time, in the fall of 1807, Thomas Jefferson heard about the failure of Pryor's expedition, he expected to hear what the Governor of Louisiana Territory intended to do about it. Months went by as Meriwether Lewis wallowed in one of his non-corresponding periods. He wrote to neither the President nor Secretary of War Henry Dearborn, who was heavily involved in Indian affairs in general and in the return of Sheheke in particular. Finally on July 17, 1808, Jefferson reached out sternly to Lewis, scolding him for his lack of communication and prodding the Governor to suggest a solution. Jefferson placed the blame for Sheheke's long exile in St. Louis squarely on Lewis.

> The misfortune which attended the effort to
> send the Mandane chief home became known to us
> before you had reached St. Louis. We took no step
> on the occasion, counting on recieving your advice
> so soon as you should be in place, and knowing that
> your knowlege of the whole subject & presence on
> the spot would enable you to judge better than we
> could what out to be done. The constant persuasion
> that something from you must be on it's way to us,

has as constantly prevented our writing to you on the subject. The present letter however is written to put an end to this mutual silence, and to ask from you a commmunication of what you think best to be done to get the chief & his family back. We consider the good faith, & the reputation of the nation as pledged to accomplish this.[104]

Jefferson, hearing nothing in response from the no-doubt embarrassed and despairing Lewis, wrote again on August 21 and 24. The president was in his last seven months in office, his term was due to expire in March 1809, and he had declared that he would follow the first president's example and serve only two terms. Jefferson had a sense of urgency to tidy up the Mandan affair. In the latter letter the President suggested that the return of Sheheke, "an object which presses on our justice & our honour," might be accompanied by a punitive expedition against the Arikara for their act in firing on troops of the United States. "I suppose a severe punishment of the Ricaras indispensible, taking for it your own time & convenience."

Lewis caught the spirit of that order. It was too late in 1808 to organize an expedition, but Lewis did finally begin to put plans into effect. Pryor had said it would take an army of at least four hundred men to return Sheheke against the opposition of the Arikara and their Sioux allies. With foreign tensions running high in the young republic, and with a president who believed in small government, an army that size just wasn't available to send up the Missouri. There were those who would volunteer, however. Commercial interest in the Upper Missouri and Rocky Mountain trade led to the formation of a volunteer militia under the direction of Pierre Chouteau, who was called Peter, presumably to make him more American, in the official documents. Chouteau, representing a new combine, the Missouri Fur Company, was contracted to return Sheheke to Mitutanka. He was to punish the Arikara on his way.

On February 24, 1809, an agreement was signed in St. Louis between Governor Lewis and the Saint Louis Missouri Fur Company.[105] In exchange for seven thousand dollars and an exclusive though very temporary license to carry on any commerce above the Platte River, the company would recruit and arm "One Hundred and Twenty five effective men, (of whom Forty shall be Americans and expert Riflemen)." They would act as an official Militia of the Louisiana Territory engaged in a campaign with the purpose of effecting "the safe conveyance and delivery of the Mandan Chief, his Wife, and child, to the Mandan Nation. . . ." The company was responsible for providing the barges to transport the militia and their human cargo. Chouteau was given specific instructions for the comfort of his guests. The company was required "to provide comfortable, and suitable accomodations on board of Covered Barges, for the said Mandan Chief, his wife, and child, and for Jesson (the Interpreter) his Wife and child, and shall furnish them and each of them with a sufficiency of Good and wholesome Provisions for their, and each of their Consumption, . . ." which sufficiency, like the accommodations, would be judged and approved by the Governor himself.

The protection of Sheheke and the rest was paramount. Lewis put into the written agreement a statement that the company "shall defend them from all Warlike and other attacks, by force of arms, and every other means to the extent of their power, and at the risque of the lives of the said detachment." Accidents and illness were to be similarly avoided, though if unavoidable tragedies occurred, the company would still receive its seven thousand dollars. Payment would be forfeit, naturally, if the company failed in its mission through its own negligence.

One clause in the contract came back to haunt almost everyone concerned. "The said Company shall safely convey such Goods, wares, Merchandizes articles, and utensils, as the Governor of the Territory shall deem necessary to send as Presents to the Indians of the Missouri, either by the said Agent Peter Chouteau, or by the said Mandan Chief."

The contract required the expedition to leave St. Louis on April 20. They had a twenty-day grace period built in, but if the company did not embark from St. Louis by May 10, they would forfeit three thousand dollars. They didn't quite make it. The first group of barges, carrying some 160 men, probably including Sheheke, left St. Louis on May 17. Others were launched a month later, but goodwill prevailed between the parties and no penalty was assessed. That goodwill was practically guaranteed between the government and the commercial interests of St. Louis, because they were the same. That is, they were the same interests and even the same people. William Clark was a partner, along with Reuben Lewis, Meriwether's brother. Manuel Lisa, Pierre Menard, Andrew Henry, Benjamin Wilkinson and William Morrison, some of the most prominent citizens of the West, were all partners, too.

The contract itself was silent on the subject of offensive actions against the Arikara, but Lewis made it clear to Chouteau that their behavior in attacking Pryor and killing members of his party was worthy of a violent reprimand. Governor Lewis sent a letter to Chouteau, dated June 8, three weeks after the first elements of the expedition had headed up the river to a staging area, a rendezvous at Cote sans Dessein, a small village of French grain farmers, hunters and fur traders. In his letter, Lewis left no room for doubt that the principal mission, the "parimount" concern for the company had to be the safe return of Sheheke to his people. He echoed the words of Jefferson, saying he considered that with the safe conveyance of Sheheke rested "the honour and Good faith of our Government . . ."[106] Nothing should be allowed to interfere with that mission and all decisions made in the field should attempt to further that end.

But, Lewis went on, "That the aricare nation should be severely Punished for their unprovoked attack on the party under the Command of Ensign Pryor in September 1807, is also devoutly to be wished, . . ." They needed to be militarily spanked, Lewis opined, for the honor of the United States and for the future safety of river commerce in the Louisiana Territory.

Anticipating by sixty-seven years the attitude of General Alfred Terry to Lieutenant Colonel George A. Custer,[107] Lewis wrote, "I deem it improper to trammil your operations by detailed and Positive Commands" regarding the mission. Unlike Terry, Lewis did go on to provide pretty detailed advice. Chouteau was to take his militia to Fort Osage[108] for inspection by the commanding officer.

They were to conduct themselves as soldiers on a war footing.

Ensign Pryor, the only American military officer who had faced the Arikara in battle, thought a force of four hundred might not be sufficient to effect the delivery of Sheheke to his home. Lewis paid attention, though he could afford to send only a militia of 125 men, only 40 of those required to be American riflemen. But he had an idea of how to build Chouteau's fighting force. Lewis suggested that Chouteau enlist friendly Indian nations to contribute warriors, to an upper limit of three hundred, as auxiliaries in a proposed attack on the Arikara villages. He expected the expedition to attract a lot of volunteer hangers-on from amongst a group of trappers, traders, and hunters, some coming from St. Louis and some who were scheduled to rendezvous with Chouteau's force at the mouth of the Cheyenne River in central South Dakota. Taken all together Lewis estimated the party would be 550 strong when it reached the Grand River villages of the Arikara.

Treatment of the Indian allies was suggested, too. Lewis was "not unapprized of the versatility of the Indian character which is always experienced in Causing them steadily to persevere in any enterprize for a length of time." He recognized Chouteau's experience and skill in dealing with Indian peoples, but couldn't resist advising him on one point, the distribution of ammunition. "I must suggest as one means of insuring their fidelity that You do not Give them an abundant supply of ammunition untill they shall arrive in the neighbourhood of the Aricares, . . ." Payment for the allies was to be all the "plunder" they could take from the Arikara.[109]

Lewis said he was open to Chouteau making peace with the Arikara and even suggested a method of determining what attitude Chouteau would take upon approach to the Grand. He should send Indian spies ahead, friends who were also friends of the Arikara, who would go to the Grand River villages and gauge the level of hostile intent. Those agents should be dispatched several weeks before Chouteau reached his rendezvous at the Cheyenne River. The spies would come back downriver to the Cheyenne to deliver their intelligence to Chouteau. If the Arikara were feeling peaceful, Chouteau was to engage them in negotiations. Peace could be bought by the Arikara giving up to American justice either the individual warriors who had inflicted fatal wounds on Pryor's party during that firefight, or, if they could not determine who had killed whom, the Arikara would be required to volunteer four men to be summarily executed by a firing squad immediately and in full view of the Arikara people. The Arikara would also give away as presents their horse herd, or at least a "suitable" portion of it, to the Indian auxiliaries accompanying Chouteau. In exchange, the Arikara would not be attacked and the unenforceable embargo on American trade with them would be lifted.

If they were not inclined to make peace on those grisly terms, Chouteau was to try to take the Arikara by surprise, "Provided you conceive you can Effect it without eminently hazarding the Primary object of the expedition, to wit, the safe Conveyance of the mandane Chief to he Village." After his first admonition about the honor of the United States riding on the safe return of the chief, and the safety of Sheheke's group being the paramount concern of the expedition, the addition of the adjective "eminently" to the prohibition against hazarding the Mandan family changes the whole perspective. That addition to the orders would lead a field commander to make a judgment about risk relative to reward. Reading this line, Chouteau would understand Lewis to be amending his orders and the contract terms. Placing Sheheke in some danger would be acceptable, if Chouteau believed he could pull off a military victory over the Arikara.

The peace proposal suggested by Lewis to Chouteau would, of course, be unacceptable to any Indian nation. Lewis, no matter how deranged he became in the months before his suicide, should have known that the Arikara would fight rather than accept the summary execution of four warriors. His years of counseling peace between the earthlodge peoples were over. The Governor of Louisiana was out for blood.

Pierre Chouteau, on the other hand, was out for business.

The second attempt to return Sheheke set out from Cote sans Dessein in late June. They spent three days at Fort Osage and continued up the river, arriving at the current site of St. Joseph,

Missouri, on July 29. They passed the Platte three days later. On August 11, Chouteau reached a village of the Omaha Nation. They were Siouan-speaking earthlodge people, as were the Mandan, but the relationship between the Omaha and Mandan had been distant at best as they had been separated by geography and demographics for centuries. With the Arikara standing between them for five hundred or more years, as were also the Lakota in the last century, the Omaha and the Mandan had a lot of catching up to do. Thirty Omaha met the boat. The principal chiefs conversed with Sheheke and invited him to visit their village. He put on his most impressive suit of clothes, an "elegant full dress suit of regimentals," and had a horse lavishly decorated for his state visit to the Omaha lodges.[110]

The Omaha had recently skirmished with the Sioux and lost several warriors. It was one battle in the long-standing war that most of the earthlodge-dwelling farmers of the Plains were fighting with the empire-building nomadic Sioux. Omaha relations with the powerful and intimidating Sioux were a matter of discussion with the American party and their Indian ally. Sheheke made a powerful impression on the Omaha, who a commentator labeled "very filthy in their dress and food." The Mandan chief, on the other hand, was resplendent in his outfit and carried himself with dignity. The whole Omaha nation, said a Dr. Thomas who accompanied the expedition, was "lost in astonishment" at the splendid figure cut by Sheheke, "so much superior to any thing their chiefs could display." Dr. Thomas was as impressed with Sheheke's attitude as the Omaha were with his clothing. In a diplomatic situation, he exuded dignity and reserve. "Shehekeh's manners would grace any circle; he took great pains to copy the manners of the first characters of the United States whom he was acquainted with."

That comment by Thomas resonates with the same tone used by other white correspondents faced with Mandan culture. Here on a personal level is the same attitude expressed by la Verendrye in saying that the impressive fortifications he saw around the Mantannes' village were not Indian. It's the attitude that drove early visitors to presume that the Mandan must be Welsh, or later writers to suppose they were descended from Christianized Vikings. If an Indian or an

Indian tribe exhibited cultured attributes, they must have learned them from the whites goes that line of thinking. Sheheke, of course, was a veteran diplomat. He didn't need to learn manners from Thomas Jefferson. His demeanor, as ever chronicled, was always dignified and gracious.

After two days with the Omaha, the party headed north again. Five days later, August 18, 1809, diplomacy became a little more difficult. Chouteau's group landed that day by a tepee village of the Yankton Dakota at the mouth of the James River. There were three hundred lodges there. Fifty warriors met the boats and carried the officers into the village on buffalo robes, six men to carry one. The American party was welcomed to a lavish feast of roast dog, with each bowl containing a single paw to leave no doubt as to the origin of the delicacy. In the council that followed the Yankton demanded that a trader be left with them and that some of the goods in the barges be distributed, post haste. The Sioux had for two years been looking for the exchange of trade goods promised to their representatives when they had visited Chouteau in St. Louis in 1807, just prior to the Pryor expedition.

Chouteau was as unwilling to give away his property to forestall violence as his son had been two years earlier, though Lewis had granted him leave to distribute presents in the interest of safely accomplishing his primary goal. Some threatening language crept into the negotiations. One Yankton said that because the waters of the Missouri were muddy the white men thought they could do as they pleased, but that if the waters ran red with white men's blood, they might treat the Yankton with more respect. Chouteau said he had no choice but to keep the goods for their intended purpose. His men were as willing to defend themselves as to make friends with the Sioux, he told the chiefs and leading men. Chouteau was an old hand in a tough business. He guessed and he was right, the Yankton was only philosophizing about the situation, he didn't intend to send the blood of these particular white men downstream. Things calmed down and a compromise of sorts was reached. The Missouri Company would establish a trading house for the Yankton, but for now the group would push on without molestation. Chouteau felt certain that it was the hospitality he extended to the Sioux delegation in St. Louis that enabled him to proceed without conflict.[111]

On August 20, they passed the Niobrara River. A band of Lakota Sioux were encountered for the first time six days later. They were flying a British flag. The same kind of conversation took place with that band of about one hundred tepees as had happened with the Yankton Dakota a week before. A trader was promised, and one was left for their convenience a few days later near the White River. Chouteau, as per Lewis' suggestion, attempted to enlist three hundred Lakota warriors for an attack on the Arikara. The Lakota declined, saying, in Chouteau's words, that "one tribe ought not to countenance any attempt to distroy another."

If that statement had any believability in 1809, it lost it over the following decades. The Lakota earned their reputation for attempting to do just that, trying to destroy other tribes for part of the nineteenth century. Fourteen years after Chouteau's trip upriver, in 1823, a band of Sioux warriors 750 strong allied with Colonel Henry Leavenworth's force for a punitive attack on the Arikara villages.[112] The Sioux, in that instance, were disappointed that Leavenworth was content with shelling the Arikara into submission rather than directly assaulting and overrunning a fortified village. In 1839, in a single battle with the Sioux, the Pawnee lost 180 men, an enormous number in a Plains Indian fight. In the spring of 1843, the Sioux boasted they would exterminate the Pawnee and killed more than two hundred of them in a series of attacks. One of the worst incidents of that type was witnessed by two American missionaries. The Pawnee village a mile from the mission of John Dunbar and Samuel Allis was attacked by several hundred Sioux warriors. Dunbar and Allis watched as the village was overrun and partially burned. Women and children were shot down as they ran from their burning lodges.[113]

But in 1809, the leaders of this one band of Lakota told Pierre Chouteau that one Indian nation shouldn't try to destroy other nations, or at least that's what he said they said in his report of the expedition to James Madison's Secretary of War, William Eustis.

Chouteau switched gears. If the Lakota wouldn't help fight the

Arikara, perhaps they would be a force for peace. He prevailed on six of the chiefs to accompany the expedition as far as the Arikara villages. With his smaller-than-hoped-for force, Chouteau was predisposed to hope for peace. It's not clear if Chouteau sent friendly agents ahead to take the temperature of Arikara feelings, as was suggested by Lewis. It seems that the militia commander did have an inkling that he could make peace. At any event, he made a play for it. His instructions from Lewis had been to launch a surprise attack, if peace on American terms was not in the offing. Chouteau clearly did not follow those instructions. Taking the Arikara by surprise wasn't possible anyway. The whole Upper Missouri knew Chouteau was coming. Even the Mandan knew Sheheke was on his way.

With a good wind allowing the use of sails on the last leg, the Chouteau party got to the villages of the Arikara on September 12, 1809, three days after the second anniversary of the Pryor fight. The Arikara were properly nervous.

Chouteau landed short of the Arikara village and arranged an encampment with a martial appearance. In the village, old men, women, and children prepared to flee. Chouteau marched his militia, with cannon, toward the village. The flotilla of barges kept pace on the river.

When the Mandan had heard that Sheheke was returning, a deputation had been dispatched to meet him. They had been waiting with the Arikara, the two nations being then at peace. A score of the leading Mandan men came out to meet the American militia. There was a general council between Chouteau, the Lakota chiefs, and the Mandan. The Lakota were the peacemakers this time, according to Chouteau. They asked for pardon for the Arikara. Chouteau would not promise peace, but suggested that the council be expanded by the attendance of the Arikara.

Four Arikara chiefs came out of the village to meet Chouteau. When he expressed surprise that so few would speak for so many, they told him that the village was alarmed by his appearance. They talked to not much purpose, and the meeting broke up before nightfall.

Chouteau was ready to talk more the next morning, but none of the Arikara came back. He sent a messenger to inquire as to their intent. Word came back that the night had passed with growing unease in the villages and now no one would come to council unless there were hostages given to the Arikara to guarantee good behavior from the Americans. The militia commander complied. Four principal men of the company went to the village. Eight Arikara chiefs went to Chouteau's camp.

When the council resumed, Chouteau chastised the Arikara for their attack on Pryor. He told them that he had orders to destroy their nation, but that the chiefs of both the Lakota and the Mandan had asked him to stay his hand. At their request he would ground his arms "until new orders can be received from your Great father who alone can pardon or destroy." Chouteau told them to bring their old men, women, and children back to their village. Then he demanded to know why they had attacked Ensign Pryor. He also wanted to know the whereabouts of the men responsible for the attack.

A Frenchman was the cause of the trouble, Chouteau was told. The French trader, a resident among the Arikara, had told them lies. He had said that the goods Pryor carried were gifts from the President of the United States, probably being offered as a form of an apology for the death of the Arikara chief traveling to the United States in 1806. So the villagers were violently disappointed when they were only given a couple of medals and the goods were retained for the Mandan, with whom they were at war. The anonymous Frenchman incited them directly, too, telling them to open fire on the Americans.

Chouteau demanded that the Frenchman be produced. But he was not available. The sole instigator was living with another band of Indians about fifty miles south. He lived there with his wife and child, the Arikara said. Chouteau repeated his demand, insisting that the Arikara send runners to retrieve the guilty party. The Indians agreed to send men along with a detachment of Chouteau's militia to guide them to the village in question. But when the time came to leave, the chosen Arikara men refused to go. Without guides, and without much real interest in what was certainly a wild goose chase, Chouteau gave up the hunt.

It needs to be noted that this account of the conversations between Chouteau and the Arikara is his account, written to the United States Secretary of War in fulfillment of his contract and militia commission. Chouteau achieved the appropriate end without bloodshed, but he felt he needed to explain why he hadn't killed anyone. He had ignored virtually every significant recommendation from the Governor of Louisiana Territory, and even after Lewis' death, Chouteau had to justify his actions. He had an answer prepared for every question.

The Arikara expressed sorrow that their relationship with the Americans had soured into bloodshed. They threw a lavish feast for the militia and encouraged the Missouri Company to establish a regular trading house near them. They explained to Sheheke that they had fired on him only because they were distraught over the death of their own chief in the United States and the principal chief of their nation was absent that September day and so unable to keep emotions and the situation in check. Sheheke was comfortable in the council. His own people had been delighted to see him and he was again conducting diplomacy on the Upper Missouri. His life was daily returning to normal as he literally and figuratively ascended. In the council, Dr. Thomas observed, "Sheheken appeared perfectly at home. He handed the calumet round the council room with all the gravity of an aginal statesman and warrior."

On September 14, 1809, Sheheke saw the Arikara villages when he looked downriver. It had been more than three years since he could do that. He was finally going home.

The countryside became ever friendlier and more familiar. After a week of fine weather the Chouteau party came upon a Mandan village, still well south of Mitutanka. Sometimes disgruntled families, unhappy with some political decision or intra-village feud, would separate from the rest of their nation. Typically the separation lasted a matter of months or, at most, a handful of years. This group had gone about thirty miles south of Mitutanka. That distance makes it less than likely that it was on the more distant Eagle Nose Butte, the traditional Village of Those Who Quarrel, which had been for centuries a place to let off steam and prevent intra-village conflict. One oral tradition repeated by Roy W. Meyer in *The Village Indians of the Upper Missouri* says that the people who had separated in this case were from Black Cat's Nuptadi Village. They were established at the Molander village site, near Price, North Dakota, according to this theory.[114] Wherever he found them, Sheheke encouraged the discontented to return home with him. They agreed to follow the chief of Mitutanka, returned from a foreign mission.

In the forenoon of September 22,[115] Sheheke returned to his city to the great pleasure of his people. As the barges swung west around the bend of the Missouri and closed on Sheheke's village, the militia fired a salute and raised the American flag. Villagers poured out to greet them, swarming over the barges and welcoming their chief, their recently malcontented, the party sent to secure his passage past the Arikara, and the American force that finally delivered on the promise to bring Sheheke home. Chouteau's militia was the strongest military force that any white nation had ever mustered on the Northern Plains. But the Mandan welcomed them without concern, almost without notice thought one insulted American, who resented the feeling that whites were being ignored in the wild rejoicing for Sheheke's return.

12

Homecoming

The chief of Mitutanka was home. He had floated away, down the Missouri, with a couple dozen Americans three years earlier and had returned with hundreds of them now. He had traveled 6,000 miles and met the President of the United States. He had counciled with the Omaha, Yankton, Lakota, Cheyenne, and Arikara, and, to top off his experience, had convinced a breakaway village to return to the fold. He had a heroic story to recount around the earthlodge fires in the coming winter. He also had a pet rooster, a Dunghill cock, among his many wonders brought from the United States. His ownership of a domestic fowl was something unique in Mandan history.

Sheheke's brother invited Chouteau and his men to a great feast of buffalo stew, corn, and vegetables. The ladies of Mitutanka had set pots on fires in lodges all over the village, anticipating the guests. Dr. Thomas noted that "our feast was seasoned by genuine hospitality." Sheheke's welcome in Mitutanka was a warm and enthusiastic celebration. Initially, on the surface, at least as seen by white observers, that was the kind of welcome he received from the entire Knife River metropolitan area. Chouteau wished to meet with all the important people in the five villages. Sheheke prepared to make the rounds with him. The chief put on his full dress uniform and accepted a fine horse brought to him for the purpose. Sheheke took his time preparing to ride his "elegant" horse, showing considerable taste, Thomas thought, in dressing him in scarlet and gold-laced housings, with a highly mounted bridle and saddle. Accompanied by thirty or forty Indians, Sheheke, Chouteau, and some of the men of the Missouri Company, their militia duties discharged and at an end, rode to the upper villages as well-armed, but well-intentioned traders.

Sheheke's return, along with his family, all in good health, evoked "the Greatest demonstration of Joy," at councils in the other villages, too, according to Chouteau. Dr. Thomas didn't see it in quite the same light, though he agreed that the welcome was a happy one. In one unidentified village above Mitutanka, the Chouteau-Sheheke party rode to the center of the village, where they waited for some time before being invited to enter a chief's lodge. It would have been a gross violation of etiquette to impose themselves without invitation. But it was similarly rude for the chiefs of the village to ignore their influential guests for any length of time.

The return of Sheheke took place during a tense time in the five villages. Le Borgne had, a few days prior, killed a prominent Mandan man in a quarrel. Now, into his presence came a serious competitor for status, Sheheke, in triumphant return from a trip the One Eye had been afraid to undertake. Sheheke, and his horse, cut an impressive swath. By his clothing, his bearing, and his highly and tastefully decorated horse, Sheheke carried himself as a figure to be admired by the residents of all the five villages. With Sheheke's career at its zenith, his influence and that of his village threatened Le Borgne's titular leadership of the region. With Le Borgne's reputation damaged by his bullying and violent temperament, and his occasional disregard of accepted social conventions, Sheheke's moment of ascendancy could be seen as real trouble for the Hidatsa chief. Le Borgne never forgave Sheheke. If the One Eye had ever respected the Mandan chief, he never did again.

After keeping Chouteau and Sheheke waiting, the Hidatsa invited them to parlay. While Sheheke attempted to maintain a dignified bearing, relishing his role as the returning hero, the Hidatsa chiefs were agitated. They were impatient for distribution of presents they thought were certain to be coming.

Those presents were wrapped up in a matter of some controversy and more bad feeling. The original contract terms, the agreement signed by Governor Lewis and Pierre Chouteau, said that the Missouri Company would deliver to "the Indians of the Missouri" whatever goods Lewis required to be sent. They would be given either as the gifts of Chouteau or Sheheke, but the generosity was really coming from Uncle Sam, represented by the Governor of the Louisiana Territory. Those intended gifts took second stage in the principals' attention to gifts for the Indian auxiliaries.

Chouteau, in St. Louis, before the expedition set out, sold gunpowder, lead, vermilion, and tobacco to Lewis, but it never left the fur trader's possession. Lewis turned it back over to him in a paper transfer for the purpose of distributing to any auxiliary warriors Chouteau might be able to enlist. If it was not used, the ammunition and trade goods were to be returned for the use of the government, or the Missouri Fur Company would repurchase the items, again from themselves in a paper transfer, but this time with money flowing from the company and back towards the United States. There was a $500 purchase followed by one for $440, for a total bill of $940 presented by Lewis to Secretary of War Eustis. Eustis refused to pay and reprimanded Lewis for failing to ask permission before indebting the government of the United States. Eustis was extremely unhappy with Lewis. Not only hadn't Lewis asked for permission to form a militia, but its purpose was no longer a priority in the office of the Secretary of War. When Lewis signed the agreement with the Missouri Company, February 28, 1809, Jefferson was still president and Henry Dearborn was still Secretary of War. One week later, there was a changing of the guard. Eustis found himself presented with a bill for $7,000 to accomplish a mission that should have been finished on Dearborn's watch. Swallowing hard and accepting Lewis' plan and budget, Eustis let the militia campaign go ahead but balked at spending any more on the same mission. He pointed out to Lewis in a letter of July 15, 1809, that "After the sum of seven thousand dollars had been advanced . . . 'the Company was bound . . . to furnish whatever might be deemed necessary for the Expedition, or to insure its success'—it was not expected that any further advances or any further agency would be required on the part of the United States."

Eustis viewed the return of Sheheke as Chouteau and his partners did, as a commercial venture. He withheld official support and even disavowed the campaign as not having the sanction of the United States. This was a hard letter, from a man holding the purse strings, and Lewis had overextended both his authority and his credit. The governor was naturally expecting to be allowed some independence of action in effecting a solution to a problem which a president of the United States had recently told him was a matter of national honor. Eustis didn't give him that much room to maneuver.

Lewis was pained. He wrote back, a little over a month later, a long letter mixing pride, outrage, self-justification, and self-pity. This was where he wrote his remembered "my country can never make 'A Burr' of me" passage. "She may reduce me to Poverty; but she can never sever my Attachment from her." The protested bills, the two for $940 and one other, also to Chouteau for other business purposes, destroyed Lewis' credit. He was forced to mortgage his Louisiana property as security. Lewis justified the additional expenditure for presents for the auxiliaries by saying that he had received, after signing the agreement, information that the expedition might face opposition from other tribes along the Missouri, including the Omaha and the Cheyenne, and of course, the Sioux. The Governor told the Secretary that he had considered it necessary to the success of the mission to make the further advance, equipping Chouteau with the ability to buy some allies. In light of the opposition Pryor had faced, finding allies could be crucial to getting Sheheke home.

Equipping Sheheke with gifts to share once he got home could hardly be considered essential to his safe return, which Lewis averred was the overriding concern of the expedition. Distribution of presents was a trader's device. It fit into the gift-giving trading culture of the Indian nations. Trades were gifts, either mutually agreed upon or unilaterally given with a secure knowledge that a gift of similar or greater worth would be returned. Lewis, though not a trader, was familiar with the importance of presenting gifts to his Indian hosts. He too often gave only medals, as far as his native friends were concerned, but he also passed around tobacco and trinkets and, to Le Borgne, a swivel gun in August 1806. Gift-giving was diplomatic, too.

White Coyote's exile from September 1807 through 1808 and into late spring of 1809 was an embarrassment to the United States. Naturally, men of goodwill like Jefferson wanted to do the right thing and get Sheheke home. But underlying the motivations was the greater political design of the government of the United States. Friendship and alliance with the Mandan and Hidatsa were important to American policy. Opening the trade route to and beyond the Knife River villages was part of a grand design to make use of and stake a claim to the upper portions of the Louisiana Territory. For this purpose, gift-giving would be required. A commercial practice became a diplomatic necessity because diplomacy aimed at commerce.

If Lewis discussed with Chouteau what items beyond blue beads would make appropriate gifts, as per the language of the written agreement, the explorer likely left some of it to the judgment of the fur trader. If Sheheke was consulted is unknown. Chouteau claimed that Sheheke had some gifts to give. That's what he said in his official report, and that's what he said at the time, too. Dr. Thomas' story agrees with Chouteau's on what would become a critical and possibly unfair view of Sheheke passed into the pages of history.

Dr. Thomas tells the story this way:

> Sheheken's conduct amused us very much. His splendid uniform and horse furniture, his fine figure, his anxiety to appear to advantage, with the contrast when compared with his brother chiefs, who appeared impatient for the presents which they expected to receive from him, were very striking objects. These articles Sheheken received from the American government, and they had rendered him, in his opinion, the greatest man in his country. It

was expected by his people that he would be pretty liberal in the distribution of some of his valuables. However, their hopes were vain: Sheheken was as anxious to retain his property, as they were to receive it. Murmurs took the place of mirth, and on our departure from the village, his popularity was on the decline.

Chouteau agreed with that assessment. "I then demanded of him the presents which had been sent by him to be distributed among these nations, he replied that they were all his own, . . ." Chouteau wrote in his report to Eustis of December 14, 1809. Chouteau's analysis matched Dr. Thomas' in that he felt it was true that when Sheheke failed to give away exceptional presents liberally in the Hidatsa village, it produced real disappointment and led to a loss of status for the returned chief.

This is a puzzling scene. Sheheke was a man noted for his generosity. He was, after all, civil chief of his village, a position conferred on men who were generous and compassionate. Sheheke had shown his generosity to the Corps of Discovery five years previous. Even if he was not generous by nature and tradition, if Sheheke was attempting to increase his stature, he knew better than to try to do that by hoarding wealth. It was to those who distributed wealth that the greatest status came.

As a mature and veteran diplomat, Sheheke knew that gift-giving was part of diplomacy. By distributing gifts from the United States to the Hidatsa leaders, in front of their own people and his, Sheheke would have strengthened the relationship between the villages. The Mandan generally, and seemingly Sheheke in particular, almost always worked for peace. Ready for war and eager for peace is a fair characterization of what is known about those people and that man. For Sheheke to refuse to distribute presents liberally that September day is to act out of type.

There are two possible solutions to the puzzle. Both require accepting some wholesale guesswork. First, it may be that there actually were no presents to distribute, other than his suit of clothes, his horse decorations, and his pet rooster. Chouteau was supposed to carry presents to be given by either himself or Sheheke to the Hidatsa. Perhaps he did not. It would be among the first times in the history of the United States, but it would not be the last time someone tried to make a buck by falsifying information about the distribution of goods to the Indians. Chouteau himself did eventually distribute presents, he said, to prevent the relations between the Mandan and Hidatsa from deteriorating further and to keep the Hidatsa leaders from feeling inferior to the splendid figure of Sheheke. The fur trader reached into the store of goods he had brought along with which to buy Indian warriors for the attack on the Arikara which had not taken place. He gave out 150 pounds of tobacco, 10 pounds of vermilion, 60 pounds of gunpowder and 120 pounds of lead balls. This, Chouteau said, seemed to restore harmony among the Hidatsa.

Chouteau's gifts did not come from the Missouri Fur Company. These were not part of the $7,000 contract, which required the distribution of presents. These presents came from the lot that was to be returned to the government if not used. Meriwether Lewis' bill for reimbursement for these items was denied, meaning that the Governor was personally on the hook for their cost. For Chouteau, giving from this stock was free.[116] Giving away the gifts specified in the contract cut directly into company profits. If Chouteau told everyone, his partners and the government alike, that Sheheke had been given goods and kept them, he could then use the goods for trade and pocket the profit. If there never had been any goods, he could cover up the bookkeeping by the same device. Chouteau had motive and opportunity to blame Sheheke for absconding with the gifts. That's one way it might have played out.

If Sheheke had in fact been given presents to distribute, another reason for Sheheke to not deliver them to the Hidatsa would be to purposefully insult their chiefs. The recent killing of a Mandan leader by Le Borgne may have required a response to satisfy the Mandan people. By withholding goods and directly insulting Le Borgne and the other Hidatsa leading men in front of a large mixed group from the five villages, Sheheke could have satisfied the national need for revenge, hoping to avoid further bloodshed. Of course, he may not have calculated that finely, but instead merely reacted as he did out of anger at Le Borgne's action. One alternative theory is advanced by some descendants as an explanation for Sheheke's alleged lack of generosity to the Hidatsa that day. They say he may have lost his societal bearings while in the United States. In those three years he was seduced into placing value on the accumulation of personal property.

In any event, Sheheke did not distribute presents to the Hidatsa chiefs upon his return to the Knife River. The Hidatsa were disgruntled about it. Chouteau made himself look good in contrast by distributing presents of vermilion, tobacco, and ammunition—gifts from the personal accounts of Meriwether Lewis.

In the end, Chouteau didn't use any more of the goods designated for the auxiliaries. Upon returning to St. Louis, Chouteau sold the remaining merchandise for $754.50 to the company of which he was a principal part. He'd given away less than $200 worth of presents in the Hidatsa village. There is no mention in the correspondence between Lewis and Chouteau, or between Lewis or Chouteau and Eustis, of any amount of presents being presented to Sheheke for distribution to his brother chiefs and friends.

After showing off his splendid new outfit and frustrating the Hidatsa chiefs, Sheheke left the Hidatsa village and returned to Mitutanka. He started to tell stories.

13

An American Advocate

On June 22, 1811, the English naturalist John Bradbury rode
into the Mandan village of Mitutanka. His party, which was
led by fur trade icon Manuel Lisa, had ridden hard that day, sticking
to the plains and separated from the Missouri's course by a range of
riverside hills. The hills protected the white men from tiny enemies.
Within the valley of the Missouri that week the mosquitoes were
unbearable to men and horses alike. Kill a hundred and a thousand
more would take their place, Bradbury complained.

Riders didn't come upon Mitutanka unannounced. Bradbury
noted that as they came into sight, the lodgetops of the village were
already crowded with curious onlookers staring in their direction.
As they entered the village to a warm welcome, every hand was
proffered for shaking in the tradition of the white nations. They
were led through the streets to the lodge of the chief, Sheheke. He
met them at the door. "Come in house," he said in serviceable if not
exactly stylish English.[117] Bradbury was surprised.

A second surprise awaited him inside the lodge. Sheheke had a
rooster. "One of the first objects that met my view on entering," he
said, was "a fine dunghill cock," which Sheheke had obtained while
in the United States.

If Bradbury was right in his conclusions, and it seems he was,

Sheheke was once again chief of Mitutanka, five years after leaving the village with Lewis and Clark and two years after his return. The fact that the visitors were immediately escorted to Sheheke's lodge, just as Meriwether Lewis had been in October 1804, indicates that the title of chief was not just honorary, but that Sheheke still held, or once again held, the status he had obtained before leaving his post.

Sheheke lit a pipe and offered it to his guests. Even before the ritual of smoking was complete, dinner was ready, causing Bradbury to speculate that Yellow Corn had started cooking when they first came in view of the village. He may have underestimated the Mandan. If indeed she was cooking for the guests and it wasn't just coincidence that the meal was ready when they arrived, she probably put on the pot when Lisa and Bradbury were still miles from the village, but under scrutiny by village scouts. They ate together a meal of jerked buffalo and pounded corn.

It had already been a long and tiring day, for the horses as well as the men. The sun was setting and Bradbury wanted to spend the night, but Lisa insisted they push on to the fur trade post on the other side of the river and seven miles to the north. They were conducted across by bullboats while the horses swam. Then the horses, who could do no more than plod along at that point in the day, walked to the little fort.

The following afternoon, at the fort Bradbury referred to as Fort Mandan, Sheheke came to visit. He was dressed in a suit of clothes brought with him from the United States. Through the translation of Rene Jessaume, Sheheke's English apparently not being quite good enough for conversation after twenty or so months of disuse, Sheheke told Bradbury something that seems today rather sad. He said he wanted to live among the whites.

"He informed us he had a great wish to go live with the whites, and that several of his people, induced by the representations he had made of the white people's mode of living, had the same intentions."[118] Bradbury doesn't record what kind of response he made to Sheheke's statement.

Before Bradbury left the area he made a final stop at Sheheke's home. Once again, Sheheke invited him in, speaking in Bradbury's tongue. He then added another word to his English vocabulary list. Sheheke looked at Bradbury "earnestly," the Englishman wrote, and said, "Whiskey?" Bradbury had not thought to bring whiskey, but he had brought gifts. He gave Sheheke some silver ornaments "with which he seemed pleased."

Sheheke aided Bradbury in a search for moccasins. After smoking, and dining on a boiled meal of jerked buffalo, corn and beans, Sheheke had a message passed along to some village women that Bradbury was interested in obtaining moccasins. The men were quickly overrun. Sheheke's lodge filled with so many women carrying so many pairs of footwear that Bradbury could buy scarcely a tenth part. He did buy a dozen pair, paying with some blue beads and red lead to be used as a paint.

There were, apparently, other people in the lodge, as well. Bradbury didn't notice, until Sheheke pointed him out, a young boy whose father had accompanied the expedition to the West Coast. Jean Baptiste Charbonneau was six years old the summer Bradbury visited the Mandan. But Bradbury could not have met "Baby Pomp" that day. Jean Baptiste was in St. Louis. It is very possible that Sheheke was referring to the child of any other man of the expedition who may have had relations with a Mandan woman during that first winter.

John Bradbury traveled that summer with Henry Marie Brackenridge, who also kept a journal of his experiences, published as *Views of Louisiana together with a journal of a voyage up the Missouri in 1811*. Brackenridge noticed a decided tension between the two prominent chiefs, Le Borgne and Sheheke. On July 4, 1811, those two happened to be with the Americans for the Independence Day celebration. Brackenridge saw Le Borgne "on one or two occasions, treat She-he-ke with great contempt." When Manuel Lisa started to recount something that Sheheke had said, Le Borgne cut him off angrily, with sarcasm, "what, does that bag of lies pretend to have any authority here."[119]

Brackenridge was left with the impression that Sheheke, who must have gained some permanent weight in the sedentary period in St. Louis, was not much of a warrior. He was also fat and too talkative, "a fault much despised amongst the Indians."

That reputation has carried through to the present. Though his family has remained proud of him and passed down stories through the generations, they still hesitate to talk too much about him publicly. The Le Borgne opinion of him has a thread of oral tradition of its own. Being too talkative and being not generous enough truly are faults at the Fort Berthold Reservation and in the wider world. The memory of Sheheke is therefore not an entirely positive one on the reservation. As the close historical ties between the Mandan and Hidatsa grew even closer after the smallpox epidemic of 1837, the political, cultural, and social distinctions between the two traditions became blurred. The Mandan view of history and the Hidatsa view of history have blended, to a large extent. Generally speaking, the fact that more Hidatsa survived the two terrible epidemics means that the Hidatsa traditions, or at least memories, predominate.

That Le Borgne called Sheheke a liar, and that Sheheke may have been characterized by some as too talkative should not unduly alarm his descendants. Le Borgne was seriously upstaged and threatened by Sheheke. The political success of the latter came at the expense of the former. Being talkative was Sheheke's business, talk was his tool of the trade. Certainly chiefs, like any speakers, were more effective when their words were crisp and well-chosen, but a lot of talk was necessary to influence public opinion in the complex inter- and intra-village political swirl of the Knife River villages in the early 1800s. If Le Borgne saw Sheheke as talking too much, it may have been that the Mandan chief talked too effectively.

It is not known if Sheheke ever left Mitutanka again. American society drew him, but whether he tried to return to the United States is not certain. What is certain is that Sheheke remained chief of Mitutanka until the day he died.

What would Sheheke have done if he had gone down the river again? He would have known, by 1811, that Captain Lewis was dead. The misadventure of returning Sheheke to his village and mounting debts and embarrassment caused by denial of reimbursement for claims submitted by Governor Lewis may have played some role in his suicide. But Sheheke also knew that Captain Clark was alive and well, or at least had been the year before. Since Bradbury came up from St. Louis after paying his respects to Clark, it is likely that Bradbury, Jessaume, and Sheheke conversed about their mutual acquaintance.

If Sheheke wanted to live among the whites, as Bradbury says he wished to do, his most logical course of action would be to seek out Clark, the Superintendent for Indian Affairs for Louisiana, and ask for his assistance. Clark had once availed himself of Mandan help. Certainly Sheheke's many kindnesses to the men of the United States would be remembered by William Clark. Unfortunately, if Sheheke did try to visit him, Clark wasn't home. Throughout most of 1812, Clark was away from his post. The reception Sheheke would have received from Clark is uncertain. What is certain is that if he went, the reception he did receive in St. Louis was inadequate. He did not receive a suitable offer to begin living among the whites, whatever that might have meant to him. Cantonment Bellefontaine had changed considerably in the years since Sheheke had been upriver. The entire old fort was abandoned to a shifting river. Only some apple trees lining the post commander's garden showed signs that the spot had been occupied. The fort had been moved up about seventy feet above its previous location. The buildings were no longer ramshackle. St. Louis was growing less ramshackle, too, and the area of the Lower Missouri was filling up with more farms and villages of the white men. In just three years, Sheheke could have noted how quickly the American frontier grew.

Perhaps Sheheke's dream was to establish a kind of Mandan consulate in St. Louis, or nearer the President. Jefferson had said he did not want misrepresentations from lying souls to come between the United States and the Mandan. The distance between them was clearly an impediment to conversation. Sheheke may have continued to hope to forge a closer and more useful alliance with the Americans. His people could have only benefited from having him serve as a resident representative to the American decision-makers. It is also possible, of course, that he simply became used to the treatment he received as a guest of the United States. For three years he hadn't been required to hunt for his family's food. Yellow Corn had not had to tend a garden. They had not had to fear attack by the Lakota or Arikara. He had developed a taste for whiskey. Maybe those motivations drove him to want to return to the United States. Maybe he was taken with its culture.

Perhaps he only wanted to visit again, not live among the whites. The translation from Sheheke to Jessaume to Bradbury's journal could make more of the statement than was actually there. Maybe he only wished to gain other eyewitnesses to verify some of the things he'd said about life among the whites.

In any event, if he went downriver again as was concluded by historian Milton Milo Quaife,[120] it was probably in the spring of 1812. Quaife held that Sheheke not only returned to St. Louis, but that he did so accompanied by a number of other warriors. On his return, he was supposedly killed by Gros Ventre (Hidatsa) or Sioux. That last part, at least, is clearly not true. If he went, Sheheke made it home safely by late-August. He couldn't have tarried long in St. Louis. In fact, if he went at all, and by what means he might have traveled is pure speculation, he set some sort of Missouri River speed record. Most likely the fourth trip to St. Louis is an unfounded fabrication.

On August 27, trader John C. Luttig saw Sheheke at the construction site later to be christened Fort Manuel, about twelve miles north of the Arikara villages near the Grand River. Sheheke and his family, along with "several of his bravos,"[121] came to trade a few robes. He was given a few items on credit. He didn't have time to repay the loan.

On October 3 word came to Fort Manuel that Sheheke was dead. Two Mandan men came to the fort with the information. A battle had taken place between the Mandan and the Hidatsa. The two chiefs of Mitutanka were killed, Little Crow along with his long-time associate, Sheheke. Three other Mandan were wounded, one eventually succumbing to the wound. The brother of Big Man held on for some time. Word of his death was received by Luttig three weeks later. The Mandan chiefs had sold their lives dearly.

Eleven Hidatsa were killed and others had been wounded, according to the Mandan reporters.[122]

The centuries-old alliance between the Mandan and Hidatsa had stretched past the breaking point. This was a major battle in Plains Indian terms. If the report was accurate and did not contain an inflated body-count of the enemy, that was a lot of death for a single fight. It was clearly not a personal or family matter. This was war between the nations, or at least between strong factions in two villages. It would be hard to patch up. Why did it happen? Why did experienced leaders like Sheheke and Le Borgne let it happen?

It was the War of 1812.

For several years, tensions between the United States and England had been high. The war with Napoleon involved an attempted British embargo on all trade with France. American ships were intercepted on the high seas, in European waters and off the North American coast. Sailors were kidnapped from those ships and pressed into British service. The international tension contributed to keeping Sheheke in St. Louis and the Arikara safe from American attack in 1808. The tensions worsened in 1812. American commerce was suffering. American pride was offended. In June of 1812, President James Madison asked Congress for a declaration of war against England. The mouse roared.

The effect of the war on the Northern Plains was to throw the fur trade into chaos. The British had come to the Plains before the Americans and had built personal and commercial relationships with the various bands. In the late summer of 1812, they carried the flag to their friends, using their contacts to encourage Indian attacks on men from the United States. At least one British agent, Robert Dickson, was busy recruiting Indian allies against the Americans in the months before war was officially declared. Word traveled from eastern Canada to the Great Plains, urging violence to expel the United States from the Upper Missouri. The suggestion was well-received. Many Upper Missouri trappers and traders were killed that fall, one by the Sioux in sight but out of rifle range of Fort Manuel. The Sioux attacked and killed trappers on another occasion, according to the Arikara. Crow warriors attacked and killed Americans.

Hidatsa Proper robbed and killed two American hunters, stealing twenty-six horses.[123] Confronted with the issue by Missouri Fur Company partner Manuel Lisa who marched to Big Hidatsa with twenty-six men, Le Borgne sent them home dissatisfied. He acknowledged the incident but refused to give up the stolen horses. The men at Fort Manuel were leery of the Cheyenne, too, though they learned that the Arikara had exaggerated when they reported that a trader from Manuel had been robbed and whipped by Cheyenne at the Cannonball. The Americans were nervous enough that they fired rounds into the dark one night, killing an Indian's dog that they had taken to be a skulking warrior.

Unrest was not confined to Indian-versus-American conflict. The Indian nations were more contentious with each other than usual, too. Some Cheyenne traders were too frightened to leave Fort Manuel without white escort that fall. They were afraid the Arikara would ambush them. The Arikara and Hidatsa were officially at war, too, though little fighting seems to have taken place. But it was the Mandan and Hidatsa who took the War of 1812 to heart. They took sides.

The Hidatsa, particularly the Hidatsa Proper and their chief, Le Borgne, were great friends to the English. Their cousins, the Crow Indians, felt the same way. The Crow, as mentioned, attacked and killed three American trappers in September. The Hidatsa had done the same to two hunters. The Hidatsa had once tolerated Lewis and Clark, but they were more generally warm to most of the British traders and very close to some. They'd thrown Evans out when he tried to end the Canadian trade. They would do the same to the Americans if it seemed appropriate and easily done. In 1812, it became appropriate, at least in the mind of Le Borgne.[124]

The Mandan, on the other hand, and Sheheke in particular, were closer friends to the Americans in 1812 than they had ever been to the British. Mitutanka had always been a second or fourth stop on the rounds of the Canadian traders. The Mandan of Sheheke's village were not as close, either figuratively or geographically, as the Hidatsa were to the British. Even when the Canadian trade was the sole source of European goods, the Mandan were more inclined toward the French and Metis of the North West Company and independent traders than they were to the more British English of the Hudson's Bay Company. On a personal scale, bringing the national issue down to the individual, Le Borgne was an Anglophile. He supported their interests. Sheheke, on the other hand, had demonstrated goodwill above and beyond the requirements of courtesy, or even friendship, during the winter of 1804–05 and in his willingness to risk all on the Captains in 1806. Sheheke was the brother of the past president of the United States. He had seen their country. He flew their flag outside his lodge. There is no doubt whose side Sheheke was on when the dispute between the Americans and the British became less than polite. Clearly Sheheke's view was the prevailing one at Mitutanka, based on the casualty report. Three names appear in the report of the battle, and all three are prominent men at Mitutanka, none from Nuptadi. The village Sheheke had lead in three decades may have stood alone that fall day in 1812. Likely it was a fight between Le Borgne's supporters among the Hidatsa Proper and the Mandan of Mitutanka who agreed with Sheheke and Little Crow. The other three villages and their warriors may have stood aloof.

There is no mention of other violence between any Mandan and Hidatsa groups through March 1813, when Luttig's journal ends. Le Borgne, in February, advocated for driving the Americans out of the country and found his position less than popular. But there were no other reports of killings of anyone by either the Mandan or the Hidatsa that winter.

But the two nations didn't quickly reconcile after the battle, either. At no time in the six months between Sheheke's death and the end of Luttig's journal did the fur trader note that he saw a party of Hidatsa and Mandan together. The Hidatsa were smoking with the Arikara and the Arikara were coming into Fort Manuel in joint parties with the Mandan. But the Mandan and the Hidatsa weren't seen together.

The War of 1812 marked a decided shift in the intertribal relations of the earthlodge peoples. The Arikara, for centuries the periodic enemy of the Mandan and their Hidatsa allies, were, in 1812 and 1813, often traveling with the Mandan to Fort Manuel. The

An American Advocate

Hidatsa and the Arikara smoked the peace pipe together three weeks after the battle in which Sheheke was killed. The Hidatsa also brought three bladders to the peace talks, gifts for the Arikara.

The late Vivian Medicine Stone of Twin Buttes, a descendent of Sheheke, said that family tradition held a different cause for Sheheke's death. Sheheke was killed, the Medicine Stones and Burrs agreed with Luttig, by the "Bigbellies," one of the bands of the Hidatsa. The Medicine Stone version involves the Arikara, too. Because an Arikara chief died while traveling with Sheheke to St. Louis or beyond, Sheheke's life was offered up by the Hidatsa as a way to keep peace amongst the earthlodge peoples.[125] It's not remembered whether the tradition refers to the Arikara Arketarnawhar who died while on a mission to Washington or to some other chief's death. It almost certainly was not the earlier incident, since Arketarnawhar's death occurred in 1806 and Sheheke died in 1812. An event that remote would be unlikely to spark national conflict and Sheheke's role in it was tenuous at the most. The Hidatsas wouldn't kill Sheheke over that.

The Hidatsa peace mission to the Arikara three weeks after Sheheke's death could be seen to support the Medicine Stone oral tradition about the Hidatsa killing Sheheke to make peace with the Arikara. But the peace initiative could also have been a natural result of war breaking out between the Hidatsa and Mandan. The Hidatsa would want to forestall any military alliance between the Mandan and Arikara directed at themselves.

This difference in perspective between the way Native American oral tradition summarizes an event and the way historians look at the same issue is something noted by Douglas R. Parks in his *Myths and Traditions of the Arikara Indians*.[126] Parks calls it an "interpersonal topical focus," the tendency to zero in on single incidents or relations between individual characters in stories to explain major historical actions. An excellent example from Parks is in the division of the Hidatsa into the Crow and Hidatsa. The oral tradition explains the split by reference to a dispute between two leading men over a single buffalo paunch. The Crow are ever after referred to along the Missouri as the Paunch Indians. To the European-influenced analyst, the reasons behind the split are clear, it was a simple division of labor, a specialization to better utilize the resources of a larger area. One group followed the herds, more or less, adopting a nomadic life in the Yellowstone country, while the other farmed on the Upper Missouri. They met at least annually to exchange the products of the chase for those of the garden. The immediate cause of the division may have been population. A single band, growing too large, might overtax the resources of an area. So the bands split along family or clan lines and eventually the divided band became two separate nations.

Likewise, from the twenty-first-century Euro-American perspective, Sheheke's death came about as an unfortunate result of the British blockade of Napoleon's Europe. To the family of Sheheke, his death was payback for the death of an Arikara chief. Both analyses could be true.

The fact that the two Mandan killed on the spot were the chiefs of Mitutanka leads to two thoughts. If not strictly coincidental, and the odds are long against that coincidence, the battle was a successful if costly assassination, or the chiefs both distinguished themselves by their valor, leading the fight and exposing themselves to the greatest personal danger. In any event, the chiefs died, surrogate soldiers in a world war, fighting for the United States, which was completely ignorant of their sacrifice.

Sheheke's body would have been recovered and taken to Mitutanka from the battle site. Yellow Corn received the news. Her forty-six-year-old husband had died in battle.

When a Mandan died in the early nineteenth century, the body would be wrapped in a buffalo hide and placed on a burial scaffold in a cemetery near the village.[127] For four days after his death Yellow Corn would sit under Sheheke's scaffold and cry for the loss, undoubtedly chopping off her hair or even removing a finger in grief. Then the dead man would be left alone. A year would go by and his body would decay. A year after his death, a Mandan's skull would be recovered and taken to what George Catlin called a "Golgotha," a shrine of skulls.[128] There Yellow Corn might care for her departed husband, packing the skull periodically with fresh sage, and coming to chat over a picnic lunch. She would tell him that White Painted House got married and had a boy the parents named Tobacco. Jessaume's children, Toussaint and Josette Therese, also found mates and married in the way of their French Catholic father.

There is a mistaken belief that Sheheke died in 1832, not 1812. The source of that theory, one repeated by as careful a historian as Donald Jackson, was Annie Heloise Abel in her editing of *Chardon's Journal at Fort Clark, 1834–1839*. In his journal entry for January 7, 1835, Chardon mentions that the day was the third anniversary of the death of a much admired old chief, The White Head. The White Head, Abel said in a footnote, was "She-ha-ka, the same who journeyed to Washington at the time of the Lewis and Clark expedition."

This is certainly wrong. The White Head is not Big White or White Coyote. If Sheheke had lived past 1812, someone would have written about it. There is a total lack of other mention of Sheheke in any known history after 1812. Further, if he had died in the winter of 1832 at the age of sixty-five, George Catlin would have mentioned Sheheke's passing, for it would have happened shortly before he arrived among the Mandan. Catlin consulted with William Clark before heading up the Missouri. Clark told him he'd be seeing some light-skinned and light-haired Indians in the Mandan villages. He would have asked Catlin to convey greetings to any of his surviving friends. Had he still been alive when winter gripped the Great Plains in 1832, Sheheke would have been on the list of people to be greeted. Catlin was at no loss for words during his Mandan retreat. The recent passing of a famous Mandan would not have escaped his notice or his pen.

No, Sheheke was dead at forty-six. He was killed in a battle with the Hidatsa, likely a casualty of the War of 1812.

14

Sheheke's Legacy

Sheheke, the White Coyote, hasn't always been viewed particularly favorably, or particularly fairly, by commentators from his own time to the present. Maybe the unkindest cut was delivered by Henry Brackenridge. "Fat," he called Sheheke, and too talkative, especially for an Indian. Le Borgne said Sheheke was "a bag of lies." Captain Clark had no complaints about Sheheke, but despite the chief of Mitutanka's best efforts, Clark liked Black Cat better, admiring the other Mandan chief's perspicacity. Sheheke's richly deserved reputation for generosity, earned throughout a lifetime, vanished in a moment, the moment when Pierre Chouteau told him to produce presents for the Hidatsa chiefs.

That series of negative comments from contemporaries and one odd incident, reported on by both Dr. Thomas and Pierre Chouteau, have colored historians' views of Sheheke. He has been seen as a minor figure in the Lewis and Clark saga and in his own world as well. Sheheke deserves better than that.

He was, all acknowledge, the principal chief of the village of Mitutanka and therefore the leader of the several bands of west river Mandan. He held that title for more than eight years, perhaps as many as twenty. While it's true that even the principal chief of a Mandan village did not wield anything approaching dictatorial authority over the independent spirits of the families and clans of his town, the position did carry heavy responsibility.

The responsibility placed on Mandan leaders was particularly heavy during the lifetime of Sheheke. Leaders are defined by their times. The greatest leaders, or at least those remembered that way, are those who steer the bullboat of state in the most turbulent waters. Abraham Lincoln, George Washington, and Franklin Roosevelt were great because their times required them to be and they rose to the occasions.

Sheheke lived his whole life in a time of crisis for his people. It was a period without precedent in his nation's history. In 1781, when he had just become a young man, smallpox reordered the strategic landscape for the lucky twenty percent who survived it. The centuries-old power of the Mandan was broken. The whole nation was reduced to refugee status. The proud Mandan were forced to accept a changed political reality. No longer able to provide for their own defense, they looked north to the Hidatsa, forging a closer alliance for mutual defense.

The alliance was a necessary accommodation, and it was, over its long history, a close and friendly relationship. The several bands of Mandan and Hidatsa eventually became one people, the Mandan-Hidatsa of the Fort Berthold Indian Reservation, joined by the Arikara after 1862. Though internally each peoples' traditions are kept alive, to the outside world the three independent nations have become officially one people, the Three Affiliated Tribes.

But in the earliest decades of the Knife River alliance between the Mandan and Hidatsa, there were tensions. The alliance was an uneasy one. Four of the five villages were each less than half the size of the fifth, Big Hidatsa, home to the Hidatsa Proper, the Menetarra. Not only were the Menetarra the most dominant people in the five villages, compared to their neighbors, they were the ones least settled into a peaceful, farming lifestyle. That more nomadic tradition contributed directly to their better survival of the 1781 epidemic.

The other bands, both Mandan and Hidatsa, were no doubt relieved to have the 450 warriors of the Menetarra on their side when the Lakota, Cheyenne or Arikara threatened. But the military support of the less sedentary and more warlike Menetarra came with the price of tension. They weren't always the best neighbors.

Sheheke's political act was played on a complicated stage. Even his own village was an amalgam. His generation of Mitutankans had grown to adulthood in five separate and very independent villages, each with its own leaders. Even when those separate villages were in existence, factionalism had been an accepted fact of life. When five became one, the factions multiplied. In all times, leaders could only lead by suggestion, consensus, and compelling oratory. There was no position in Mandan history appropriate to describe as a ruler. The Mandan were not willing to be ruled. Sheheke rose to the highest position of his culture, but still had authority, even within his village, only in proportion to his persuasiveness.

Beyond his own village, Sheheke's role in that pan-village society of the Knife River metropolitan area was probably always a matter of some debate and shifting status. Black Cat was a more significant leader, the "Grand Chief of the Mandans," to Clark,[129] and he and other correspondents from the Mandan-Hidatsa villages acknowledged the power of the Hidatsa Proper leader Le Borgne.

This lack of status, to some, could explain Sheheke's willingness to risk everything on the potentially status-enhancing exploration of the United States. The men who turned Lewis and Clark down, Black Cat and Le Borgne, had already achieved enormous status among their peoples. They had no higher rung to climb. Sheheke did, according to this way of thinking.

The fact is that Sheheke was truly a chief. He was a principal chief of his village, the civil chief of Mitutanka. Lewis and Clark conferred the title of chief on men of importance. They used informants and their own eyes to determine status among the people they met. Sheheke was one of the first to earn the title when he hosted them in his village on October 26, 1804. They called him a chief then, likely because he was one. Stephen Ambrose places him as the Grand Chief of the Mandan[130] who met Lewis and Clark on that island by Yellow Earth Village. If that was him, on October 24, then he was leader, for that day at least, of twenty-five warriors and their lodges. The Arikara chief who traveled with Lewis and Clark presumably would have known something about the leadership structure of the nations with whom he had so often fought and then negotiated. The Arikara Arketarnawhar is a likely source for Clark's information that he was meeting the Grand Chief.

Clark called him the First Chief of his village in 1804. He had been told who was chief where by Black Cat the day before. Seven years later, despite having been absent for nearly half the intervening years, Sheheke is a chief still, according to John Bradbury. Not only is he a chief by Bradbury's definition, but he is treated like a chief by his village. Bradbury's delegation is directed, by the hand-shaking crowd, to the chief's lodge, where Sheheke greets him in English, "Come in house." He had been more than warmly received by his own village upon his return from St. Louis. Not only had he done something no other Mandan or Hidatsa had done, but he capped off his long exodus with a diplomatic coup, bringing the dissenting lodges home with him. The people presented him with a fine horse finely dressed. His brother threw a feast in his honor upon his return. He was still a chief two years later. Sheheke was not lacking in status in his village.

What Sheheke was not was a particularly dominant figure in the five villages. In that larger area, he was coach or co-coach of an undersized team. The many warriors that Le Borgne could muster from his Big Hidatsa Village, plus his able diplomatic abilities, gave the Hidatsa leader a dominant position in the five villages. Le Borgne was pre-eminent, but he was not chief of the 4,000 residents of the five towns, because there was no such position. There was no structure overarching the five villages, as each was distinct for a reason. They were separate bands of people who had traveled different paths to the Knife River villages. They had separate histories. They did not have a pan-village council to determine issues. They acted in concert, when they did, because it made good sense to stick together and because orations and discussions led to some degree of consensus.

Le Borgne's words would not have carried the weight of Sheheke's in the lodges at Mitutanka, but he was much more able to direct events swirling around the five villages because he carried the biggest stick. Any competition in status between the two men would be wrapped up in a larger competition between their villages. Le

Borgne's Hidatsa Proper living in their Big Hidatsa Village had the greatest collective influence among the five village groups, making Le Borgne's influence the greatest. He was also a fierce warrior and a skilled and fearless diplomat. He was loyal to his friends and developed a reputation among the North West Company men as someone reliable and influential. Le Borgne, the One Eye, was the principal man of the five villages. Sheheke did not equal him in inter-village status, except perhaps briefly on that day of his return.

Black Cat was much respected by Clark. The Mandan had "more integrety, firmness, inteligence and perspicuety of mind than any indian I have met with in this quarter." He called him, repeatedly, the Grand Chief of the Mandan. From the American perspective he led the entire Mandan Nation. That was a good thing, they thought, because "with a little management he may be made a usefull agent in furthering the views of our government." But Black Cat's Grand Chiefdom was an illusion. He did lead the village of Nuptadi, but as there was no inter-Mandan governing body spanning the two remaining villages, he had no opportunity to claim leadership of Mitutanka. The Mandan villages, according to archeologist Ray Wood, "were in fact all but totally politically autonomous in spite of the ceremonial symbols of tribal unity."[131] There was no such thing as a Mandan state. There were only independent villages, and Sheheke was an important man in one of them and Black Cat was important in the other.

Likely, in 1804, there were still vestiges of the seven villages to be found even within both Mitutanka and Nuptadi. Neighborhoods may have clustered like the Mandan survivors of the epidemic of 1837 clustered within the coalesced Mandan-Hidatsa village of Like-a-Fishhook. Leaders and sons of leaders from different bands had merged their interests but would not have lost their voices. Leadership among the Mandan was awarded by merit and exercised by persuasion. Black Cat was the leader of the Nuptadi, or east river Mandan who lived in the village of Nuptadi. Black Cat was an elder statesman who was both willing to discuss economics and geopolitics with the Americans, as he was, in the words of James Ronda, "exploring the explorers."[132]

Though Lewis and Clark believed Black Cat to be the overall leader of the two Mandan villages, and perhaps of the other Mandan lodges in a third village, they treated Sheheke more frequently as if he were a true decision-maker. After hearing that a party of Mandan had been attacked by Sioux, it was to Sheheke that Clark went with an offer of military assistance. Clark marched his men across the frozen Missouri, drawing up in military order on the plain behind the village, creating quite a stir. Sheheke came out to see what was up. They discussed the situation in Sheheke's lodge, eventually agreeing that a winter chase involved too much risk for too little reward.

Later, when Lewis determined after another incident to go after the violators of his preposterous edict that the nations of the Northern Plains must all live in harmony, he had word sent to Mitutanka, that is, to Sheheke. A party of Sioux had roughed up some of his men and Lewis was intent on punishing the guilty and recovering the goods. Sheheke was one of a handful of Mandan who came to offer comradeship. He offered to fight alongside the Americans.

Sheheke's closeness to the Americans, his willingness to join them in conversation, in hunting, in war and, finally, in the exploration of their country, was the result of his commitment to his people and his own geographical and economic background. It was both a noble act and a calculated deed that promised great potential benefits for his village, with little risk, the potential loss of just one talkative politician and his family.

Sheheke had always lived on the southern frontier of friendly territory. Born and raised in On-a-Slant, his village had been last in line for driftwood, floating buffalo in the ice-clogged Missouri, and for traders from the north and west. The Hidatsa had always been closer to their relatives, the Crow, the dominant tribe to the west. They were a little geographically closer, too, when the Crow followed the Yellowstone and Missouri to the earthlodge villages. The Assiniboine and later the Canadians, excluding Jessaume, became closer allies to the Hidatsa than to the Mandan. Trade to the south, even travel to the south, had always been difficult because of the hostility of the Lakota, Dakota, and Arikara. Sheheke grew up knowing their war parties could be just over the hills southwest of On-a-Slant. He was now chief of the village closest to the enemy.

When John Evans came up the river with his tales of Spanish

agents, goods, and military forces coming, the people of Mitutanka probably liked what they heard, at least until Evans mentioned the embargo on trade with the north. That edict doomed Evans. Hidatsa relations, especially, were good with the British traders from Canada. If Evans' story of Jessaume's attempts to have him killed is reliable, the Mandan were Evans' salvation. Mandan leaders refused to do Jessaume's bidding and then a Mandan interpreter protected him, warning Evans that Jessaume was leveling a gun at him. Jessaume had more to lose from the Evans position than anyone. He was the Mandan specialist of the decade. He was married into a Mandan family. The Hidatsa disposition toward the northern men assured traders that they would be welcomed, no matter what Evans' adopted king proclaimed. The North West Company men and the Hudson's Bay men who traded with the Hidatsa wouldn't be overly concerned. But Jessaume would be. The Mandan were more likely to look south, if there were a reliable supplier to be found there. He needn't have worried about Evans. When he ran out of goods, he was evicted from the five villages. In later years, Black Cat would remember Evans as a liar. Sheheke doesn't mention him.

There were qualitative and quantitative distinctions between Evans' visit and that of Lewis and Clark. The boats and the amount of goods and men they could carry were widely different. The Americans built their own fort and demonstrated more serious resolve through their military bearing. They apparently had bulled their way upriver through the many nations that lived below while Evans more likely slipped by the Arikara villages at night and was fortunate not to draw the attention of the Sioux. People who could force their way upriver might be reliable suppliers. Sheheke considered the possible benefits of a water-born trade route to the south. There had been nothing like it in the Mandan world, other than the Canadian's use of the Souris and Assiniboine Rivers. The Souris was forty miles from the Missouri. The water route to the south ran right by Mitutanka. Sheheke's village was the closest of the five to St. Louis.

Beyond the trade possibilities, Sheheke saw the potential usefulness of having a powerful friend to the south. It could do no harm and could only help to have an ally on the other side of Arikara and

Lakota country. The strength of the Americans, right in his own country, wasn't lost on the Mandan chief either. From the first, Sheheke had maneuvered to gain good-neighbor status with the Americans. He wanted the benefit of a close relationship with Lewis and Clark because it would make trade easier, and because forty extra guns was a significant addition to local defense. The Mandan rumor mill sprang into action, too. Rumors were spread to discourage Hidatsa visits to Fort Mandan. The Mandan rumor mill was a loose form of government action in the loosely organized government. Twice in la Verendrye's ten-day visit to the villages of the Mantannes, he heard rumors that had the goal of influencing the six hundred Assiniboine visitors to leave once they had exhausted their trade potential. Whether the Mantannes were the Mandan or the Hidatsa, the technique was clearly in use along the Missouri. It is certain that the Mandan did use the technique on the Hidatsa in 1804. The Mandan, according to the Hidatsa, had spread a rumor that the whites were dangerous to the Hidatsa, that they were very angry with the Hidatsa and had allied with the Sioux in planning an attack on the Hidatsa. Evidence cited included the military bearing of the Americans, their sentries, and the moving of the white interpreters and their families into Fort Mandan.[133] The Mandan and Sheheke wanted the Americans as their allies and partners to the exclusion of the Hidatsa. They were seeking to change the balance of power in their metropolitan area.

Sheheke went to Washington because he thought he could help his people. To say his motivation was to seek personal status is akin to saying a government official is doing a good job so that people will vote for him. It doesn't generally hurt one's status to attempt something noble. Sheheke's act was noble. It was perhaps more daring than the exploration undertaken by Lewis and Clark. They traveled with an armed band of their countrymen, fellow soldiers on a mission with a clear chain of command. Sheheke put himself and his family totally in the hands of foreigners.

Epilogue

History is poignant. All the characters in all the stories from the nineteenth century and before share one thing in common: they are all dead. Many of the lead characters in the Lewis and Clark story died shortly after their brush with history. Lewis took his own life in an inn on the Natchez Trace in Tennessee in 1809. Sheheke died near home, in a battle with former allies in the fall of 1812. Sacagawea died of putrid fever at Fort Manuel ten weeks later. Others died later, or their deaths were unnoted by history. Black Cat's death is lost to both history and the memory of those who live today on the Fort Berthold Indian Reservation, according to James Ronda.[134] His death is hidden behind the smallpox curtain of 1837, beyond which oral traditions were lost. Moments from his life are recorded in the pages of the Lewis and Clark and LaRocque journals. Yellow Corn's death is similarly unrecorded. Only her face remains, in the St. Memin drawing, and the briefest of glimpses into her relationship to Sheheke. Charbonneau lived until 1835, still in the company of young Indian wives.

But, history, though poignant, is also redeeming in its way. All those men and women are dead, but so are all the others who lived in their times. Only the names of a few—usually the most interesting and influential—are remembered. If Sheheke disappoints modern sensibilities by asking if his guests have brought whiskey, he also provides inspiration with his courage to strike off into the unknown, through known dangers, with a group of men from an alien culture.

The Mandan were explorers. Lydia Sage-Chase, a descendant of the last Mandan Corn Priest, tells a story that goes with lower back therapy. She has a cylindrical block of a very light wood, maybe eight inches long with a diameter of two inches or less, which she uses as a massage tool for aching bones and muscles. The story that comes free with the therapy concerns the origin of that particular kind of wood, a healing wood that grows far to the south in the country of "the Men-who-eat-men." The Mandan occasionally traveled to that dangerous land along the Gulf Coast because they prized the healing properties of the wood so greatly. When they did, Sage-Chase says, they would time their arrivals to coincide with a trading period when the Men-who-eat-men observed some dietary restrictions.[135]

Other tales put Mandan trading parties on the trail to Hudson Bay. They ranged many hundreds of miles from the Pembina River to the Rockies. But no Mandan to his time, in legend or record, ever returned from travels as distant, geographically or culturally, as did Sheheke in 1806 and 1807. His family, in the stories told to Vivian Medicine Stone, make him a bi-coastal visitor, going to the Pacific as a teenager and to the Atlantic as a chief.

Sheheke, Shahaka, Big White, White Coyote, Shek-sho, She-heg Shoat, Great White Wolf, Grand, the Mandan Chief, all the names he was known by, is a footnote in history. But during his lifetime he was the most famous man that had ever lived in North Dakota. He was a brave man, probably a flawed man, and a remembered man. His family remembered him. To them, Lewis and Clark played bit parts, a little confused in the oral tradition.

> One day a white man came up the river with a boat in which there were thirty others; part of whom rowed and part of whom pulled the boat by a rope. They were very tired and those pulling the boat had sore shoulders. No one welcomed them so White Coyote invited them to his tepee, gave them food and cured their sores.

> When they were all rested they decided to go no further. The white man asked White Coyote to go to Washington with him. He consented and took his wife and young son; then about two years old. His wife's name was Yellow Corn. They stayed away for several years, and when they brought them back the

Rees fired on the boat and drove them back. A year
later a boat with soldiers and a big American flag
came up the river.[136]

Sheheke's son, White Painted House, learned English very well
during his most formative years. He was around two years old
when he accompanied his mother and father to meet Thomas
Jefferson. He was about five when he returned. His name can as
easily be translated as Lodge Painted with White Clay, a name given
by his aunt, who kept her house in that manner. Sheheke's son lived
to be about fifty-six years old, dying in 1860.[137] In 1832, he had a
son, Tobacco, who married a woman with the same name as his
great-grandmother. Tobacco and Beaver Woman had two sons,
named Lonefight and Gun that Guards the House.[138] Gun that
Guards the House was born in 1852. He received Sheheke's peace
medal and still told stories of his great-grandfather into the twenti-
eth century.[139] Lonefight's son was named Ted Lonefight, Sr., whose
daughter was Vivian Lonefight Medicine Stone, whose daughter is
Diana Medicine Stone, whose daughter is Vivian Hurkes.[140]
Tobacco and Beaver Woman had a daughter, too. Her name was
Eagle Woman, and she married Sam Jones. Their daughter
Charlotte had a daughter whose name was Bernice, whose son was
Valerian Three Irons.[141] The Wounded Faces also descend from, and
remember stories about, White Coyote. But, even if Sheheke had
left no progeny, or his line had died out with his son, his legend
would have lived on. A footnote to history, perhaps, but a footnote at
least. Another footnote is the Jefferson Peace Medal given to
Sheheke. According to Paul Russell Cutright, who studied that topic
in the 1960s, the Sheheke medal was handed down "to such Mandan
descendants as Good Boy, Four Bears, Four Turtles, Red Buffalo
Cow, and Black Eagle, until it finally came to Burr Crows Breast
who sold it to Dr. Kenneth O. Leonard of Garrison, North Dakota."
That's a very curious story, and one contradicted by a number of
sources. The really curious part is in the beginning. Good Boy and
Four Bears making the list of implied descendants of Sheheke.
Perhaps Good Boy and Sheheke were related. Maybe Four Bears was

a nephew of Sheheke. Maybe Cutright didn't get it right.

As long as the story of Lewis and Clark is told, Sheheke will be part of it. "If we eat, you shall eat," he said. As long as there is a Mandan Nation, he will be remembered, and as long as there is a United States, he should be honored for what he did. Foreign men did much for the young United States. The Marquis de Lafayette, General Von Steuben, and Tadeusz Kosciusko get some mention for their contributions. Sheheke has gotten much less, but he was very helpful to an important American initiative at the dawn of the nineteenth century.

Imagine the alternative. What if the Mandan had not been the people they were, with their well-earned reputation for hospitality? If Sheheke had been cynical about the new American presence on the Upper Missouri, or, worse, if he had been hostile to the advances of the United States, because he saw into the future of reservation life for his people and therefore opposed the expedition, it would have been a failure. The friendship of the Mandan and their willingness to trade large quantities of food for small pieces of metal meant that the Corps of Discovery could accomplish their work and stay healthy through the bracing North Dakota winter.

Sheheke was key to the reception Lewis and Clark did get, long before he stepped into the pirogue with Clark in August 1806. "If we eat, you shall eat," he said, and he meant it, and he could deliver on it. The Corps of Discovery ate. The other Mandan believed as Sheheke did and were quick to make friends with the American party. The Hidatsa, though, had a different focus. Their orientation was to the north. The mission of the Corps was clearly contradictory to the status quo, a status quo that the Hidatsa found quite comfortable.

If the Mandan had not been so forthcoming with corn, life would have been difficult, even dangerous, for the Americans. A simple embargo on trade from the Mandan and Hidatsa would have, in all likelihood, been deadly.

But Sheheke assured the strangers from the south that, "If we eat, you shall eat." These are powerful, gracious words from an American hero from another nation. The Northwest Corps of Discovery landed in a good place.

Endnotes

[1.] Russell Reid, *Lewis and Clark in North Dakota,* State Historical Society of North Dakota, Bismarck, 1948, reprinted 1988, page 342.

[2.] G. R. Will and H. J. Spinden, in their vocabulary of the Mandan, *The Mandans, A Study of Their Culture, Archaeology, and Language*, Papers of the Peabody Museum of American Archeology and Ethnology, Harvard University, Volume III, Number 4, 1906, write the word for prairie wolf, or coyote, as Ceheke. The word for white is shown as cote or cotte. His name has been often pronounced Shag-sho, or Shahek-shote to the author by Mandan and Hidatsa associates.

[3.] "... the Fort Lincoln site which evidence shows was completely destroyed by fire." George Will comments in *A History of the Mandan and Hidatsa*, Alfred E. Bowers draft Ph.D. dissertation to the University of Chicago, State Historical Society of North Dakota, Bismarck, page 3.

[4.] Stan Ahler's conclusion, based, among other factors, on the absence of trade goods in the site's earliest eras of occupation, is that the village was founded around 1575, "it could be AD 1525 or AD 1550 rather than 1575, but it is almost certainly no later than AD 1575." *Archeology of the Mandan Indians at On-a-Slant Village*, Northern Arizona University, Flagstaff, 1997, page 97.

[5.] Earthlodge village sites have at least two and often three names in addition to their archeological designations. They each had a name, maybe more than one, in the Mandan language. These are often lost to memory. They may have a second name as a translation in English. These names are often indicative of some feature of a site, like On-a-Slant, or Double Ditch, which actually has four ditches and the name of which in Mandan translates as Yellow Earth, or Yellow Clay Village. If neither of those types of names is available, the recourse has been to name them for their locale, as is the case with Huff Village, a National Landmark near the town of Huff, or Motsiff, Sperry, Larson, and Boley, all named for their local landowners.

[6.] Alfred E. Bowers, *A History of the Mandan and Hidatsa*, a draft of his unpublished Ph.D. dissertation, State Historical Society of North Dakota, Bismarck, page 80 and footnote to page 80.

[7.] Ibid, page 179.

[8.] Donald J. Lehmer, *Introduction to Middle Missouri Archeology*, Anthropological Papers I, National Park Service, Washington, 1971, page 128.

[9.] University of North Dakota archeological field school dig, 2001, author communication with Dr. Dennis Toom.

[10.] Henry Haxo, translator, "The Journal of La Verendrye," *North Dakota Historical Quarterly*, Volume VIII, Number 4, State Historical Society of North Dakota, Bismarck, July 1941, page 263.

[11.] It should be noted that there is some question as to whether Sheheke was referring to seven villages all on the west side of the river as Mandan and ignoring the two on the east side as belonging to another people. It is this author's belief that he was not and that there were in his youth seven villages, not nine, that modern observers would characterize as Mandan. The number of villages in existence at any one time is a topic for a book all its own.

[12.] Diana Medicine Stone e-mail to author, January 3, 2003.

[13.] Elliot Coues, editor, *The Manuscript Journals of Alexander Henry and of David Thompson*, Ross and Haines, Minneapolis, 1897, reprinted 1965, page 326.

[14.] Duncan Strong field notes, Smithsonian Institution, Washington, D.C.

[15.] Gilbert Wilson, *The Hidatsa Earthlodge*, published in the Anthropological Papers of the American Museum of Natural History, Volume XXXIII, Part V, The American Museum of Natural History, New York, 1934, page 366.

[16.] George Catlin, *Letters and Notes on the Manners, Customs, and Conditions of North American Indians*, London, 1844, reprinted by Dover Publications, New York, 1973, page 82.

[17.] Author conversation with Louella Young Bear, Fort Berthold Community College, New Town, February 1994.

[18.] Colin F. Taylor, *Catlin's Okeepa*, Verlag für Amerikanistik, Wyk auf Foehr, Germany, 1966, page 61.

[19.] Alfred E. Bowers, *Mandan Social and Ceremonial Organization*, University of Chicago Press, Chicago, 1950, pages 124–125.

[20.] Taylor, page 78.

[21.] Ibid, page 59.

[22.] Ibid, George Catlin's remarks on plate number 6, page 138.

[23.] Catlin, page 97.

[24.] Lehmer, pages 97–105. Lehmer suggests that Extended Middle Missouri groups from North Dakota contested for and won control of the Big Bend region of South Dakota, displacing Initial Middle Missouri groups with whom they likely shared a parent stock centered in southern Minnesota and northern Iowa in the twelfth century.

[25.] Larry J. Zimmerman, *Peoples of Prehistoric South Dakota*, University of Nebraska Press, 1985, page 108. Zimmerman discusses the Crow Creek massacre and mass burial of at least five hundred villagers in the fourteenth or fifteenth century.

[26.] Reid, page 343.

[27.] Bowers, *History*, page 20.

[28.] John C. Ewers, editor, *Indian Art in Pipestone: George Catlin's Portfolio in the British Museum*, Smithsonian Institution Press, Washington, 1979, page 52 footnote.

[29.] Ibid.

[30.] Bowers, *History*, page 22.

[31.] Ibid, page 85.

[32.] John C. Jackson, "Brandon House and the Mandan Connection," *North Dakota History*, Volume 49, Number 1, Winter 1982, State Historical Society of North Dakota, Bismarck.

[33.] Author conversation with Stanley Ahler, North Dakota Heritage Center, November 2001.

[34.] Author conversation with Raymond Wood, Sheraton Hotel, Colorado Springs, October 2002.

35. Others have estimated smaller numbers. This estimate is based on thirteen earth-lodge villages with populations ranging from 1,000 to more than 3,000 per site.

36. Ahler, *Archeology*, page 94.

37. John C. Jackson.

38. Ibid.

39. Elliot Coues, editor, *New Light on the Early History of the Greater Northwest: The Manuscript Journals of Alexander Henry the Younger and of David Thompson*, 1897, reprinted by Ross and Haines, Minneapolis, 1965, Volume I, pages 337–338.

40. Baptiste Good's Winter Count, copy in Fort Abraham Lincoln Foundation Interpretive Division.

41. Bowers, *History*, page 155.

42. Maximilian, Prince of Wied, *Travels in the Interior of North America*, Ruebon Gold Thwaites, editor, Volume II, The Arthur Clark Company, Cleveland, 1906, page 361.

43. *Dictionary of Canadian Biography*, Volume III, 1741 to 1770, University of Toronto Press, page 246.

44. Ralph S. Thompson, "The Site of the Mandan Indian Village Visited by Verendrye in 1738: A New Look," *North Dakota History*, State Historical Society of North Dakota, Bismarck, Fall 1984, pages 22–28. This article proposes that la Verendrye most likely visited the Larson site, a Mandan village on the east side of the Missouri north of Bismarck.

45. Haxo, page 263.

46. Richard M. Deacon, *Madoc and the Discovery of America: Some New Light on an Old Controversy*, George Braziller, Inc., New York, 1966, page 217 footnote.

47. Mary Lile Benham, *La Verendrye*, Fitzhenry & Whiteside, Don Mills, Ontario, 1980, page 52.

48. Bob Saindon, "LaRocque," *We Proceeded On*, The Lewis and Clark Trail Heritage Foundation, Inc., Helena, Montana, May 1987, pages 4–10.

49. Ibid.

50. A. P. Nasatir, editor, *Before Lewis and Clark, Documents Illustrating the History of the Missouri, 1785–1804*, Volume I, St. Louis Historical Documents Foundation, St. Louis, 1952, page 76.

51. L. R. Masson, editor, *Les Bourgeois de la Compagne du Nord-Ouest*, Aniquarian Press Ltd., New York, 1960, page 272.

52. Nasatir, page 97.

53. Ibid, page 462.

54. Ibid, page 463.

55. Ibid, page 327.

56. Ahler, page 16, and author conversation with Loren Yellow Bird in Charlottesville, Virginia, January 19, 2003. Arketarnawhar or Ank-e-douch-a-ro, names by which Is-a-Whippoorwill, or Was-to-ne, has been known, are various pronunciations for the word meaning "chief" in Arikara.

57. Bowers, *Mandan*, page 34.

58. Ibid.

59. James P. Ronda, "Exploring the Explorers," *Great Plains Quarterly*, Spring 1993, Volume 13, Number 2, Center for Great Plains Studies, Lincoln, 1993.

60. Carol Lynn Macgregor, editor, *The Journals of Patrick Gass: Member of the Lewis and Clark Expedition*, Mountain Press Publishing, Missoula, Montana, 1997, page 73.

61. Stephen Ambrose says this is Sheheke, and a case could be made for that. It's not clear, however, from the journals that it is Sheheke. Clark calls him "one of the Grand Chiefs." Later in his journals he refers to Sheheke as a Grand Chief. Clark also repeatedly calls Black Cat "Grand Chief of the Mandans."

62. Gary E. Moulton, editor, *The Journals of the Lewis and Clark Expedition*, Volume III, University of Nebraska Press, Lincoln, 1999, page 200.

63. This is a presumption based on Lewis and Clark seeing Sheheke as first chief. Lewis would assume he was being taken to their leader. Also, Bradbury was taken to Sheheke's house seven years later.

64. David Thompson's estimates of the number of lodges and hence the population of the five villages is at considerable variance from the estimates given seven years later by William Clark. The differences in lodge numbers for Mitutanka are by far the greatest, with Thompson seeing 113 lodges there and Clark reporting only 50. Thompson also counted only 82 lodges at Big Hidatsa. A smallpox epidemic that supposedly hit the Mandan in 1800–01 (R. G. Robertson, *Rotting Face: Smallpox and the American Indian*, Caxton Press, Caldwell, Idaho, 2001, pages 194–197) might be seen as the cause of the reduction at Mitutanka, but even if the poorly documented epidemic struck the Mandan then, which is by no means certain, it doesn't explain the disappearance of more than half of the village's lodges, while the other villages maintained population, or in the case of Big Hidatsa, grew in size.

65. Moulton, page 234.

66. Ibid, page 268.

67. Reid, page 128.

68. The "Medicine Stone" of Clark's journal is probably the Medicine Rock of Medicine Rock State Historic Site, south of Elgin, North Dakota. The rock, though not on any map to discourage vandalism, is still visited by Native Americans on spiritual quests. Most often today, perhaps exclusively, it is Lakota Indians who visit the site to pray and fast and study the rock's petroglyphs.

69. Donald C. Jackson, *Letters*, Thomas Jefferson to C. F. C. Volney, February 11, 1806, page 291.

70. Raymond Wood and Thomas D. Thiessen, editors, *Early Fur Trade on the Northern Plains, Canadian Traders Among the Mandan and Hidatsa Indians, 1738–1818,* Table I, University of Oklahoma Press, Norman, 1985.

71. Coues, page 344.

72. Catlin, page 96.

73. Reid, page 327.

74. James P. Ronda, "St. Louis Welcomes Lewis and Clark," *Voyages of Discovery*, Montana Historical Society Press, Helena, Montana, 1998, page 204, contains the list of toasts. The quote from Ronda is from *We Proceeded On*.

75. Ibid, page 205.

76. Jackson, *Letters,* page 325.

77. Richard Dillon, *Meriwether Lewis: A Biography*, Coward-McCann, Inc., New York, 1965, page 265.

78. Ibid.

79. Stephen E. Ambrose, *Undaunted Courage: Meriwether Lewis, Thomas Jefferson and the Opening of the American West*, Simon & Schuster, New York, 1996, page 418.

80. Jackson, *Letters*, page 351.

81. *Thomas Jefferson: Indian Addresses*, "To the Coyote and People of the Mandan Nation," Washington, December 30, 1806, reprinted from The Avalon Project: wysi-wyg://129/http://www.yale.edu/lawweb/avalon/jeffind5.htm.

82. Bowers, *History*, page 163.

83. Ellen G. Miles, *Saint Memin and the neoclassical profile portrait in America*, National Portrait Gallery and Smithsonian Institution Press, 1994, pages 146–147.

84. Dillon, page 267.

85. *The National Intelligencer*, December 31, 1806.

86. *Universal Gazette*, January 22, 1807.

87. *The National Intelligencer*, January 16, 1807.

88. Jackson, *Letters,* page 373.

89. Ibid, page 382.

90. Ibid, page 412.

91. Ibid, page 414.

92. Ibid, page 306.

93. Ibid, page 743.

94. Ibid, page 303.

95. Ibid, page 433.

96. Ruth Beebe Hill, *Hanta Yo*, Doubleday & Co., Garden City, New York, 1979, page 21. Based on the Elk Winter Count, with reference in the Long Dog Winter Count. In two separate winter counts, references are made to Red Shirt being a Lakota chief and to his wounds being caused by two arrows.

97. Carolyn S. Denton, "George Shannon of the Lewis & Clark Expedition: His Kentucky Years," in George B. Yater and Carolyn S. Denton, *Nine Young Men from Kentucky*, We Proceeded On Publication Number 11, National Lewis and Clark Trail Heritage Foundation, Inc., May 1992, second printing June 2000.

98. Rene Jessaume, Missouri Historical Society, translation of a letter from Rene Jessaume to Thomas Jefferson, December 3, 1807, St. Louis, 236.

99. Jackson, *Letters*, page 435.

100. Kate L. Gregg, "Building of the First American Fort West of the Mississippi," *The Missouri Historical Review*, Volume XXX, Number 4, State Historical Society of Missouri, Columbia, July 1936, page 353.

101. John Francis McDermott, "St. Louis as Military Headquarters," *Bulletin*, Volume XXIII, Number II, Missouri Historical Society, St. Louis, January 1967, page 108.

102. Frederick Bates letter to George Rogers Clark, December 1807, Bates Family Papers, Volume 2, Missouri Historical Society, St. Louis, page 153.

103. *We Proceeded On*, National Lewis and Clark Trail Foundation, Inc., Helena, Montana, February 1994, page 15.

104. Jackson, *Letters*, page 444.

105. Ibid, page 447.

106. Ibid, page 452.

107. Terry's last orders to Custer read, "the Department commander places too much confidences in your zeal, energy, and ability to wish to impose upon you precise orders which might hamper your actions when nearly in contact with the enemy." From Donald Horn, *Portrait of a General: George Armstrong Custer and the Battle of the Little Big Horn,* Don Horn Publications, West Orange, New Jersey, 1998, page 64.

108. Jackson, *Letters*, page 452, referred to by Lewis as "fort Clark."

109. Ibid.

110. Donald C. Jackson, "Journey to the Mandans, 1809; The Lost Narrative of Dr. Thomas," *Bulletin*, Volume 20, Number 3, Missouri Historical Society, St. Louis, April 1964.

111. Jackson, *Letters*, page 480.

112. Douglas R. Parks, *Myths and Traditions of the Arikara Indians*, University of Nebraska Press, Lincoln and London, 1996, page 11.

113. Colin G. Calloway, "Army Allies or Tribal Survival: The 'Other Indians' in the 1876 Campaign," a paper delivered at the 1994 Little Bighorn Symposium in Billings, Montana, published in *Legacy: New Perspectives on the Battle of the Little Bighorn*, Montana Historical Society Press, Helena, 1996, page 69.

114. Marilyn Hudson, Administrator of the Three Affiliated Tribes Museum, June 21, 2002, letter to Betty Morgan.

115. Jackson, "Journey," page 190. Dr. Thomas says September 22, but Jackson, *Letters*, page 484, citing the *Missouri Gazette* of November 16, 1809, says September 24.

116. It turned out that it wasn't free for Chouteau, though he couldn't have known at the time. When Lewis' letter of exchange was rejected by Secretary of War Eustis, Chouteau, the endorser, became obligated to make it good. He described, to Eustis, the use of the goods as "to obtain the free passage of the mandan chief and to replace the presents announced and promised to his nation, which had not been forthcoming." Pierre Chouteau Letterbook, English translation, Missouri Historical Society, St. Louis, page 113.

117. John Bradbury, *Travels in the Interior of America in the Years 1809, 1810, and 1811*, Sherwood, Neely & Jones, London, 1819, reprinted by University Microfilms, Inc., Ann Arbor, 1966, page 138.

118. Ibid, page 143.

119. Henry Marie Brackenridge, *Views of Louisiana: Together with a Journal of a Voyage up the Missouri, in 1811*, Cramer, Spear and Eichbaum, Pittsburgh, 1814, reprinted by Readex Microprint Corporation, 1966, page 261.

120. Fred L. Lee, "Sha Ha Ka: Lewis and Clark's Mandan Indian Friend," *The Trail Guide*, quarterly publication of the Kansas City Posse of the Westerners, Volume XII,

September 1967, Number 3, Kansas City, page 19.

121. John C. Luttig, *Journal of a Fur-Trading Expedition on the Upper Missouri 1812–1813*, edited by Stella Drumm, Missouri Historical Society, St. Louis, 1920, pages 73–74.

122. Ibid, pages 82–83.

123. Richard E. Oglesby, *Manuel Lisa and the Opening of the Missouri Fur Trade*, University of Oklahoma Press, Norman, 1963, page 130.

124. Ibid, page 122. Le Borgne urged war against Americans, according to Luttig's journal of February 21, 1813. His position, the trader said, was controversial and Le Borgne had lost some popularity among his people.

125. Author telephone conversation with Diana Medicine Stone, Bismarck, North Dakota, May 2002.

126. Parks, page 100.

127. At least that was the method employed by the 1830s. Below-ground burials were used in some earlier periods, as evidenced by numerous burials found in cache pits in Heart River Phase village sites, and by the words of Dipauch, who, when asked by Maximilian why the Mandan did not bury their dead, responded, "The Lord of Life has indeed told us that we come from the ground, and should return to it again; yet we have lately begun to lay the bodies of the dead on stages, because we love them and would weep at the sight of them." Maximilian, 1906, page 361, quoted by William Duncan Strong in *From History to Prehistory in the Northern Great Plains*, Smithsonian Miscellaneous Collections, Volume 100, page 363.

128. Catlin, pages 90–91.

129. Moulton, Volume III, page 242.

130. Ambrose, page 183.

131. Raymond C. Wood, *An Interpretation of Mandan Culture History*, Reprints in Anthropology, Volume 25, J&L Reprint Company, Lincoln, 1982, page 13.

132. James P. Ronda, "Exploring the Explorers: Great Plains People and the Lewis and Clark Expedition," *Voyages of Discovery: Essays on the Lewis and Clark Expedition*, Montana Historical Society Press, Helena, 1998, page 183.

133. Ambrose, page 188.

134. Author conversation with James P. Ronda, San Diego, October 2001.

135. Author conversation with Lydia Sage-Chase, Twin Buttes, North Dakota, September 1994.

136. Calvin Grinnell paper presented at Fort Abraham Lincoln State Park, Nu'eta Corn and Buffalo Festival, August 3, 2002, citation from "The Story of a Medal related by its owner, Gun That Guards The House," Volume II of the Collections of the State Historical Society of North Dakota, Bismarck, 1908.

137. Ibid.

138. Medicine Stone e-mail.

139. Paul Russell Cutright, "Lewis and Clark Indian Peace Medals," *Bulletin*, Volume XXIV, Number 2, Missouri Historical Society, St. Louis, January 1968, pages 165–166.

140. Medicine Stone e-mail.

141. Author conversation with Valerian Three Irons, 2001.

References

Ahler, Stanley A. *Archeology of the Mandan Indians at On-a-Slant Village.* Flagstaff: Northern Arizona University, 1997.

Ahler, Stanley A. and Thomas D. Thiessen and Michael K. Trimble. *People of the Willows: The Prehistory and Early History of the Hidatsa Indians.* Grand Forks: University of North Dakota Press, 1992.

Ambrose, Stephen E. *Undaunted Courage: Meriwether Lewis, Thomas Jefferson and the Opening of the American West.* New York: Simon & Shuster, 1996.

Badertscher, Patricia M. *An Archaelogical Assessment of Star Mound.* Draft prepared for the Archaeology and Native Heritage Commitee, Manitoba Heritage Council, February 1995.

Bates Family Papers, Volume 2, Missouri Historical Society, St. Louis.

Benham, Mary Lile. *La Vérendrye.* Don Mills, Ont.: Fitzhenry & Whiteside, 1980.

Bowers, Alfred W. *Mandan Social and Ceremonial Organization.* Chicago: University of Chicago Press, 1950.

—. *A History of the Mandan and Hidatsa.* Unpublished dissertation at the University of Chicago, 1948, copy provided by the State Historical Society of North Dakota.

Catlin, George. *Letters and Notes on the Manners, Customs and Conditions of North American Indians.* London, 1844, reprinted by Dover Publications, New York, 1973.

Chardon, F.A. *Chardon's Journal at Fort Clark 1834-1839.* Lincoln: University of Nebraska Press, 1997.

Coues, Elliot, ed. *The Manuscript Journals of Alexander Henry and of David Thompson.* Minneapolis: Ross and Haines, Inc., 1897, reprinted 1965.

Deacon, Richard M. *Madoc and the Discovery of America: Some New Light on an Old Controversy.* New York: George Braziller, Inc., 1966.

Dictionary of Canadian Biography, Volume III, 1741–1770, and Volume VI, 1987, University of Toronto Press.

Dillon, Richard. *Meriwether Lewis: A Biography.* New York: Coward-McCann, Inc., 1965.

Ewers, John C., ed. *Indian Art in Pipestone: George Catlin's Portfolio in the British Museum.* Washington, D.C.: Smithsonian Institution Press, 1979.

Fenn, Elizabeth A. *Pox Americana: The Great Smallpox Epidemic of 1775–81.* New York: Hill and Wang, 2001.

Flandreau, Grace. "The Verendrye Overland Quest of the Pacific." Reprinted in *The Quarterly of the Oregon Historical Society,* Volume XXVI, Number 2, June 1925.

Gregg, Kate L. "Building of the First American Fort West of the Mississippi." *The Missouri Historical Review,* Volume XXX, Number 4, July 1936.

Historical Overview of Fort Clark State Historic Site, North Dakota. Report prepared for North Dakota State Parks and Recreation Department and the State Historical Society of North Dakota, December 1999.

Horn, W. Donald. *Portrait of a General: George Armstrong Custer and the Battle of the Little Big Horn.* West Orange, NJ: Don Horn Publications, 1998.

Jackson, Donald C. "Journey to the Mandans, 1809; The Lost Narrative of Dr. Thomas." *Missouri Historical Society Bulletin,* Volume 20, Number 3, April 1964.

—. *Letters of the Lewis and Clark Expedition with Related Documents 1783–1854*. Second edition. Urbana and Chicago: University of Illinois Press, 1978.

Jackson, John C. "Brandon House and the Mandan Connection." *North Dakota History*, Volume 49 Number 1, published by the State Historical Society of North Dakota, Winter 1982.

"The Journal of La Verendrye, 1738–39." Translated and annotated by Henry E. Haxo. Reprinted in *North Dakota Historical Quaterly*, Vol. VIII, No. 4, July 1941.

Krause, Richard A. *The Leavenworth Site: Archaeology of an Historic Arikara Community*. University of Kansas Publications in Anthropology, Number 3, 1972.

Lehmer, Donald J. *Introduction to Middle Missouri Archeology*. Anthropological Papers 1, published by the National Park Service, Washington, 1971.

Luttig, John C. and Stella Drumm, ed. *Journal of a Fur-Trading Expedition on the Upper Missouri 1812–1813*. St. Louis: Missouri Historical Society, 1920.

MacGregor, Carol Lynn, ed. *The Journal of Patrick Gass*. Missoula: Mountain Press Publishing Company, 1997.

Masson, L. R., ed. *Les Bourgeois de la Compagne du Nord-Ouest*. New York: Antiquarian Press Ltd., 1960.

Maximilian, Prince of Wied and Reuben Gold Thwaites, ed. *Travels in the Interior of North America*. Volume II. Cleveland: The Arthur H. Clark Company, 1906.

McDermott, John Francis. "St. Louis as Military Headquarters." *Missouri Historical Society Bulletin*, Volume XXIII, Number II, January 1967.

Miles, Ellen G. *Saint Memin and the Neoclassical Profile Portrait in America*. Washington, D.C.: National Portrait Gallery and the Smithsonian Institution Press, 1994.

Miquelon, Dale. *New France 1701–1744*. Toronto: McClelland and Stewart, 1987.

"Missouri River Boats." Exhibit Handout Number 88–2, published by the State Historical Society of North Dakota, Bismarck.

Morton, Arthur S. *A History of The Canadian West to 1870–71*. Toronto: University of Toronto Press, 1973.

Moulton, Gary E., ed. *The Journals of the Lewis and Clark Expedition*. Lincoln: University of Nebraska Press, 1999.

Nasatir, A. P. *Before Lewis and Clark, Documents Illustrating the History of the Missouri, 1785–1804*. St. Louis: St. Louis Historical Documents Foundation, 1952.

Nester, William R. *The Arikara War, The First Plains Indian War, 1823*. Missoula: Mountain Press Publishing, 2001.

Oglesby, Richard Edward. *Manuel Lisa and the Opening of the Missouri Fur Trade*. Norman: University of Oklahoma Press, 1963.

Reid, Russell, ed. *Lewis and Clark in North Dakota*. Bismarck: State Historical Society of North Dakota, reprinted 1988.

Robertson, R. G. *Rotting Face: Smallpox and the American Indian*. Caldwell, ID: Caxton Press, 2001.

Ronda, James P. *Lewis and Clark among the Indians*. Lincoln: University of Nebraska Press, 1984.

—. "Exploring the Explorers." *Great Plains Quarterly*, Spring 1993, Volume 13, Number 2, Center for Great Plains Studies, Lincoln, 1993.

—, ed. *Voyages of Discovery*. Helena: Montana Historical Society Press, 1998.

Saindon, Bob. "LaRocque." *We Proceeded On*, published by The Lewis and Clark Trail Heritage Foundation, Inc., Helena, May 1987.

Schneider, Mary Jane. *North Dakota's Indian Heritage*. Grand Forks: University of North Dakota Press, 1990.

—. "Cultural Affiliations of Native American Groups within North and South Dakota: An Ethnohistorical Overview." Report to the Dakotas Area Office, U. S. Bureau of Reclamation, Bismarck, 2002.

Stewart, Frank H. "Mandan and Hidatsa Villages in the Eighteenth and Nineteenth Centuries." *Plains Anthropologist*, Volume 19, Number 66, 1974.

Snortland-Coles, Signe. *Boley Site (32MO37) and Mandan Burial Customs*. Bismarck: State Historical Society of North Dakota, 1987.

Split Rock Studios. *Fort Clark and Mitu'tahakto's Trade, Tragedy, and Transitions, 1830–1860*. First Draft of final text for the Sheldon Gallery of the Lewis and Clark Interpretive Center in Washburn, North Dakota, 2001.

Steinbrueck, E. R. *Selections from Steinbrueck's Note-Books On the Mandans, 1905–1907*. Bismarck: State Historical Society of North Dakota, undated.

Strong, Duncan. Field notes. National Anthropological Archives, Smithsonian Institution, Washington, D.C.

Taylor, Colin F. *Catlin's Okeepa*. Germany: Verlag für Amerikanistik, Wyk auf Foehr, 1966.

The National Intelligencer, December 31, 1806 and January 16, 1807.

Thomas Jefferson: Indian Addresses. "To the Coyote and People of the Mandan Nation." Washington, December 30, 1806. Reprinted from The Avalon Project: wysiwyg://129/http:www.yale.edu/lawweb/avalon/jeffind5.htm

Thiessen, Thomas D. "An Early Visit to On-A-Slant Village." *North Dakota Archaeological Association Newsletter*, Volume 22, Number 3, Anthropology Research, Grand Forks, October 2001.

Thompson, Ralph S. "The Site of the Mandan Indian Village Visited by Verendrye in 1738: A New Look." *North Dakota History*, published by the State Historical Society of North Dakota, Bismarck, Fall 1984.

Universal Gazette, January 22, 1807.

Will, G. R. and H. J. Spinden. "The Mandans, A Study of Their Culture, Archaeology, and Language." *Papers of the Peabody Museum of American Archeology and Ethnology*, Harvard University, Volume III, Number 4, 1906.

Wilson, Gilbert. "The Hidatsa Earthlodge." *Anthropological Papers of the American Museum of Natural History*, Volume XXXIII, Part V, The American Museum of Natural History, New York, 1934.

Wood, W. Raymond. *An Interpretation of Mandan Culture History*. Reprints in Anthropology Volume 25. Lincoln: J & L Reprint Co., 1982.

—. and Thomas D. Thiessen, eds. *Early Fur Trade on the Northern Plains, Canadian Traders Among the Mandan and Hidatsa Indians, 1738–1818*. Norman: University of Oklahoma Press, 1985.

Yater, George H. & Carolyn S. Denton. *Nine Young Men from Kentucky*. Great Falls, MT: Lewis and Clark Trail Heritage Foundation, Inc., 1992.

Zimmerman, Larry J. *Peoples of Prehistoric South Dakota*. Lincoln: University of Nebraska Press, 1985.

Index